Québec is Killing Me

HELENE JUTRAS

Québec is Killing Me

Translated by Helene Jutras & Michael Gnarowski

THE GOLDEN DOG PRESS
OTTAWA—CANADA—1995

©English translation, THE GOLDEN DOG PRESS, 1995

ISBN # 0-919614-59-0
Canadian Catalogue in Publication Data

JUTRAS, HELENE
Québec is killing me

Translation of: *Le Québec me tue.*
ISBN 0-919614-59-0

1. Quebec (Province)—History—Autonomy and independence
movements. 2. Quebec (Province)—History—Autonomy and
independence movements—Social aspects. 3. Quebec (Province)—
Politics and government—1994- 4. Quebec (Province)—Social
conditions—1960—I. Gnarowski, Michael, 1934-II. Title.

RC2925.2.J8813 1995   971.4'04   C95-900662-1
R1053.2.J8813 1995

To Chris.
With my eternal gratitude to Thanh-Tram.

"The tie that binds you to your family is not one of blood but of respect and joy in the life of each member. It is rare that members of the same family grow up under the same roof."

Richard Bach
Illusions or The Adventures of a Stubborn Messiah.

BY WAY OF A FOREWORD

In the late summer of 1994, and, more specifically on the
30TH of August and, almost a month later, on the 27TH of
September, the venerable Montreal daily Le Devoir which
has long and loyally served the cause of Québec national-
ism, published two thoughtful articles entitled "QUÉBEC IS
KILLING ME".

The election campaign (destined to be won by Mr.
Jacques Parizeau and the sovereigntist Parti Québecois)
was dragging painfully, and a jaundiced press seemed to
have run out of things to say. Publication of the two articles
provoked a public outcry and a deluge of correspondence
the likes of which had not been seen by Le Devoir in years.
As a matter of fact, nothing like it had occurred since the
debate around Bill 178 which had restricted severely the
use of English on public signs and displays.

Radio and television immediately took up the issues
which I had raised, and the argument has continued for
months in the press. All of this has meant a certain notoriety
for me, and I have appeared and have been interviewed on
four television shows and two radio programmes, and have
been the subject of profiles in two major Montreal dailies.

I hasten to sound a note of warning for the reader who
may be expecting grand solutions to our problems but will
find only a detailing of those issues which I think need to
be addressed and critiqued. As a matter of fact I believe
that if solutions can be found they are likely to be lodged
in the problems which have exercised us. In other instances
we may have to be patient, since many of the points I raise
are part of the age-old mentality of Quebeckers as well as
of much of humanity, and changes of that order are slow
and require much work and great dedication to change. To

achieve the latter, however, it is imperative to recognise our problems, and not to hide our heads ostrich-like in the sand. It will not be easy to start a debate in Québec society without provoking the usual anguish which has attended such initiatives in the past. We have been too long inclined to the habit of keeping quiet in the hope that our difficulties will disappear on their own rather than to confront them head-on and to ask searching questions for which we expect honest answers.

I do not claim to represent my generation. Only too often one lumps people in groups saying "the young generation" as if we are all the same simply because we are of the same age. This is silly. Many of those who would be opposed to my ideas may very well be of my generation, while those who may be in sympathy may be as mature as my parents. I would also like to say that I do not offer my ideas as being those of a special group, nor, for that matter, do I wish to blame anyone in particular. I find that one falls easily into ther trap of blaming that generation which has been labelled the baby boomers. They are no guiltier than anyone else. They too have had their difficulties just as I will have mine, and that's all there is to it. They wanted to do well and if things haven't quite worked out we can, of course, blame them, but we must also blame those who have continued to pursue the same objectives. Moreover, I do not see what the benefit would be, and I certainly refuse to make people feel guilty if only because it has been done to me too frequently. At the same time I believe that all individuals must take responsibility for their actions or lack of it. This is not putting the blame on anyone; it is simply being realistic

There is a tendency to confuse the young with that

which is called Generation X, but I as a young person reject being lumped into something for which I have no definition, especially if what is implied suggests the idea of an attitude of "no future". If, however, what is meant is a generation which because of its variety of attitudes and ideas is indefinable, I would find this an acceptable characerization, although I continue to deplore the labelling of generations which I see as an ongoing and unwelcome tendency in our society. Thus when my reflections appeared in Le Devoir I found myself rolled into one with my generation and described variously as wimps, whiners and near-imbeciles, an act of gross generalisation which suggests a low level of tolerance and understanding.

The purpose of this discourse is not to put forward a social or political analysis or, for that matter, any other kind of analysis of Québec. Some readers have criticized what they describe as "a lack of depth in my analysis". That is of course the case because it was not my intention to attempt an analysis. I wanted to express my own opinion and feelings as they apply to the present situation. If an analysis is called for, it will follow, but for the moment I do not have any such aspirations. Some may have interpreted what I have had to say as an attempt at a profound critique worthy of a doctoral dissertation. If that is the case they have misread my drift, and I would like to remind them that language has many subtleties, and that I am not quite the basket case that they led themselves to believe from a superficial sense of the title of my essay. Let them really master the nuances of the language that they flatter themselves in believing that they truly know.

I have never claimed that my ideas are that new or that original, only that they express things that we have pre-

ferred to forget or to hush up. For those who have accused
me of a lack of originality I say that even Molière bor-
rowed from Plautus and no one complained. But ours is a
very different time. We are madly in pursuit of things new,
always wanting the new, while the Greeks of antiquity
were only too happy to spend hours listening to the great
stories of the past which they knew by heart. Today the
ordinary man and woman uses the pretext of lack of time
to excuse their lack of learning and the shallowness of their
sensibility. If what I am saying is well-known to you, do
not put it aside, but rather ask yourself why it is still necessary to be saying the very same things that we have
known and have been saying since the days of the Quiet
Revolution? Why is it that nothing has really changed? I do
not pretend to have the answers, but I do know one thing:
This stagnation, it is the fault of us all.

LETTER PUBLISHED IN LE DEVOIR ON AUGUST 30, 1994.

It has been an unavoidable fact of life that every few months a news topic returns to the headlines. You will see that this business will be back before the 12TH of September. For example, this or that opinion poll reports that young anglophones in the Province of Québec are seriously thinking of leaving in the course of the next half dozen years. We, the readers, are surprised. As a matter of fact we are shocked at this news and we want to know why this is happening and how can it be prevented. But no one thinks to ask young francophone Québeckers what they are thinking. Nobody asks them how they view their own future prospects in the Province of Québec, and whether they too may be thinking of making their lives elsewhere. The traditional collective mentality of Québec assumes that because Québec youth was born in Québec and has its roots in Québec, it will stay here and die here. We have raised around these youths the walls of a ghetto of expectation, walls that are as high as human stupidity and narrow-mindedness can make them. Why does someone not ask them if they would like to leave Québec? I think that the answer would surprise many.

In my own case, I will soon turn nineteen. I was born in Québec and I have grown up here. In September I begin my studies in Law. Would you like to know what is my dream? (Yes, I can still dream.) And what do I dream of? Simple things. I dream of a nice house, a child, a dog, and a good well-paying job. Nothing out of the ordinary, but I believe that I will not be able to realize this dream in Québec. And so, just like my anglophone contemporaries, I want to leave. I want to go to the States or to Europe, or wherever, but most of all I do not want to stay here.

I cannot realately explain why I want to leave, at least not without offending the majority of the population. To put it simply, I feel suffocated. They say that the population of Québec is aging. I believe it, and although I am young and have my whole life ahead of me, somehow I feel very old. There, I have said it. I still have my dreams, but my ideals vanished about the time that I turned fifteen. It was much too early to lose them. I no longer believe in the intelligence of human beings since I have seen too many fools taken for geniuses. I no longer believe that one day Québec will be independent, although, for a long time this hope was like the promise of fresh air, the promise of renewal. I have come to realize that nothing will change because our people are the way they are. Indecisive and not very proud or sure of themselves. So I look to the south and think that we can say anything we want about the Americans (Yes, they are mad and violent, whatever you may choose to make of it), but you cannot take away from them their pride in themselves. And us, what can we say for ourselves? I'll say it. We are occasional Québeckers. We take our flags and our costumes out of the closet on the 24TH of June[1], and we engage in all the hoopla of parades, and we play the songs of Gilles Vigneault[2] and the old lyrics of Paul Piché[3]. But, I ask you, what remains of all this on the 25TH? I, myself, no longer celebrate the holiday of Saint Jean on the 24TH. It is too depressing.

[1] The 24th of June is the feast day of St. John the Baptist and has been celebrated as a national holiday by French Canadians from the earliest days of settlement. It has now become a rallying date for Québeckers of an independentist persuasion.

[2] Gilles Vigneault popular singer and composer probably best known for his song "Mon Pays" which has become a kind of unofficial anthem of the independentist movement in Québec.

[3] Paul Piché a popular Québecois singer of decidedly nationalist inclination.

Of course, there are young people of my generation who are interested in politics although I do not pretend to understand them. As a theoretical exercise I find politics interesting, but in a practical sense, for example the present electoral campaign,[1] I find the exercise boring to say the least. I do have some strong ideas about how we could improve things. First of all, I would make it illegal for political candidates to abuse and criticize one another. What is the use of criticizing one another when the time would be much better spent in expressing and prompting new ideas in which one believes than in wasting time running down one's opponent. Perhaps if the politicians were more inclined to keep their peace we would have a chance to get at the little bits and pieces of truth that survive in their speeches.

In any case, politics comes down to the charisma of the leader of the party. This was as true of René Levesque as it was true of Pierre Elliott Trudeau. Take away this idea of charisma and you are reduced to the kind of debate that is presently unfolding in Québec. The people will be forced to elect a leader whom they dislike least, and this may prove not to be an easy choice.

If the liberals win it will be more of the same. There are no jobs, there is no money, and the deficit is not going down. If the Parti Québecois wins, then it's war. They will not be able to create more jobs, nor will there be more money, and, definitely, the deficit will not go down. The only thing that we will have will be more squabbles and confrontation with the federalists threatening us with a loss of pensions, and the "separatists" as our Prime Minister

[1] The provincial electoral campaign which saw the defeat of the provincial Liberals under Daniel Johnson, and brought Jaques Parizeau and the Parti Québecois to power in Québec.

likes to call them, trying to defend themselves as best they can. But all in vain, and we will be the first people in human history to have refused twice in the span of fifteen years the opportunity to take our destiny into our own hands. I am ashamed even to think of the prospect.

In 1839-1840, Lord Durham wrote a report[1] on the francophone community of Canada. According to him, the English invaders had only to wait and the francophones would disappear. The Church thwarted this plan by encouraging backwardness and the growth of a Catholic population. I know that I simplify things here, but what I say is essentially true. At the same time I do not know if the Church and its Clergy really did us a favour. We have been left with a feeling of inferiority vis à vis the rest of the world, and by believing that one is a fool one becomes a fool.

Certainly, it may be said that because of this attitude the French language has survived in North America, at least that is what they say. Nevertheless I recently met a young Québecoise who is the product of twelve years of our school system who could not distinguish between the verb "to be" and the verb "to have". Again, I was ashamed of our system of education that has so neglected reading that it produces intellectually handicapped freaks unable to think analytically or to analyse a simple phrase like "Rover is a beautiful dog". And yet I say we cannot expect the system to do everything for us. One expects an element of intellectual curiosity that would complement our schooling. And yet—although I do not know the answer to this—

[1] The "report" in question was made public in the Parliamentary Papers of the British Parliament in 1839, and its text was published in London, Montréal and Toronto in the same year. It was not exclusively "sur le peuple francophone" as the author implies in her text, but, as its title clearly indicates, a "Report on the Affairs of British North America" with sections on Lower Canada (Québec), Upper Canada (Ontario) and the Atlantic Provinces.

this intellectual curiosity, essential though it may be, is a rare commodity.

I, of course, do not have the capacity to change things, and I also know that people will hold these criticisms against me. Already when I speak of moving away to live elsewhere eyebrows are raised and there is incomprehension. This is the mentality shown so well in *Les Belles Soeurs,*[1] where if anyone shows the ability to better himself he is held back. An attitude worthy of the Middle Ages.

My departure, of course, would not change anything in Québec, but it would improve my life, just as letting the world know that I dream of leaving will not change anything. Except, that I am not alone. I am convinced that nothing can be done to stop the growing outflow of young Québeckers who are following, more and more, in the footsteps of artists and entertainers like Robert Lepage (who was ignored in Montreal until he scored an international success), and the exodus of well-off pensioners who flee to Florida to escape a climate of which I do not even want to think. There is nothing to be done, we can only wait and watch as Québec bleeds quietly. One asks, "Who will be left to pay the pensions of the last hangers-on?"

---

[1] Les Belles Soeurs (1968), best-known play by Québecois playwright Michel Tremblay. Written in joual, it is characterized by the depiction of weak and loutish male characters and blowsy women portrayed in an all-too-familiar working class setting into which Tremblay himself had been born.

Letter published in Le Devoir on September 27, 1994 .

I am fed up. I have said it often enough that I want to leave Québec. I have said that our politics are taking us nowhere, and that I certainly did not have the capability to change anything, and, predictably I have been attacked for saying it. So, I will stop saying these things and I will try to explain why I see our situation as I do.

I have been accused of being a defeatist, of being a pessimist. I challenge this notion by inviting those who would criticize me to prove to me with concrete examples that my vision of Québec life is wrong-headed. I say that Québec is dying because, little by little, its people are becoming stupider. Those things which I value:—knowledge, intellectual development, are not found here. Culture belongs to the well-to-do, and no effort is being made to teach ordinary people to appreciate it. And please, do not tell me that it is the same everywhere. The popular theatre of Bali which so attracted and intrigued Artaud[1] is a theatre that comes from the people and is an art form that is in touch with the spiritual values that inspire the Balinese. Our "ordinary people", on the other hand, gravitate to the lighthearted humour of summer theatre where the great appeal is that it does not demand great intellectual effort. And so, if culture begins to slip and serious theatre collapses for want of an audience, we blame the educational system for not teaching French to our youngsters. These are idle excuses: if French is losing ground it is because Québeckers do not care enough to learn it properly, and let us not blame our leaders for this. Culture does not depend on politics, it

[1] Antonin Artaud (1896-1948), French poet and theatre personality whose experimental theories, particularly his idea of the "theatre of cruelty" which was intended to startle and disturb the audience, influenced drama in the 1920's.

depends on the will of the people. It is the people who create culture just as it is the people who neglect it and, ultimately, who make it die.

They tell me that the grass is not greener elsewhere. But I say that in certain instances it may very well be greener. Sure, the economy is in crisis as it is everywhere in the world, but the difference is that everywhere else in the world the people have an identity. Unlike Québeckers, they know who they are and they are not preoccupied with this question, while we hesitate and seem not to know. And because we do not know, we lack confidence in ourselves and are going nowhere.

It is also apparent to me that my ideas have been taken for a political message. Perhaps, in a limited sense it is so since politics seems to be at the heart of everything, but at the same time, it is useless to lay all the blame on politics for things gone wrong because of a lack of change in our affairs. Politicians are not magicians. They end up by saying what people want to hear, because, in the final analysis politics is a popularity contest which is won by those politicians who are closest to public opinion.

It becomes obvious, therefore, that only a change in the people will produce a corresponding change in our politics and not the other way around. It is for this reason that I claim that it makes no difference for which party we vote, since we may change leaders but the people will remain the same with its insecurities and its mental laziness. The people have great power but they prefer not to use it. The people of Québec are like a big child who refuses to grow up. We may place its destiny in its hands, but it will prefer to do nothing rather than risk the consequences of action. Its mother loves it well but is becoming exasperated at a child who will leap in the river to avoid getting wet in the rain! And imagine the embarrassment if Mother Canada threw the child out of the house thus forcing it to be what it already is. Would it return to cry in Mama's skirts? In saying this I do not want to leave you with the idea that I am a staunch independentist. Quite the opposite, I don't believe in independence any more, and I would hope sincerely that we stop talking about it and not run the risk of new ridicule. It is compromise that, politically, is killing Québec. I wish that we would decide once and for all and stop talking about second options.

In an article published on the 24TH of September, a Mr. Pascal Brissette said that it is simplistic to believe that independence will solve the problem of the young and not so young leaving Québec. Really, it is just self delusion and while it is true that the plan of the Parti Québecois will give hope to some it will not make up for the inadequacies of our people. The Romans had their own way of distracting the people with bread and circuses, we have our own project of sovereignty which is rapidly running out of steam. In both instances it is the same result: the people are entertained and for a little while they forget that they are starved. The coming referendum will occupy people for a while, and imagine if Québec were to become sovereign... Mr. Parizeau's "project for a new society" will preoccupy us for some time. But what then? After ten years? Are we going to be a more evolved and open society genuinely interested in art and the sciences? I do not think so. Appearances will have changed but the essence of Québec will remain the same. Independence should come as the result of a process of growth and development in the sensibility of the people, while it is being offered to us as some kind of miraculous solution with no foundation upon which to base it and nothing to back the facade.

Since I am constantly bombarded with political exhortations, I am going to state it bluntly: My vote is null and void. I had once planned to vote for the Parti Québecois in the hope that "one never knows maybe it will end this debate". I changed my mind when I heard Mr. Parizeau talk of suspending a fifty dollar fee for CEGEP[1] students who had accumulated five or more failures in one semester on their record. This is not something that touches me personally since I no longer attend a CEGEP. But when I was a student at that level I passed every single course because I worked and because I wanted to learn and to succeed. I do not see why those who are slackers should not be expected to pay for their attitude. Attending a CEGEP is not mandatory. It is a free choice that one makes guided by the spirit of advancement and self-improvement. Those who go to college to fool around get in the way of others who are eager to learn. And that is the problem of Québec. We bring things down to the level of the least accomplished and the weakest, and make no provision to enhance the advancement of those who aim to succeed. This is a policy which is responsible for the brain drain from which we suffer. I understand that Mr. Parizeau's decision was politically motivated and that he was hoping to gain votes from college students which may or may not work to his advantage. I am incensed, though, that he even made such a promise. Ignorance may reign in Québec, but must we deify it?

Over the years we have erected an elaborate system which makes it possible for us always to blame someone

[1] CEGEP stands for Collège d'enseignement générale et professionel and represents a level of post-secondary education equivalent to the community college in the rest of Canada.

else for our difficulties. We are like big, spoiled children. Even the brightest among us get caught in this trap. The government, the educational system, our parents (always our parents) , their parents and their parents' parents before that, all of them are blamed a hundred times a day. We drag them before the bar of the accused, and we condemn them without benefit of appeal. It is they who have not taught us to write properly; and they who do not govern well. And it is they, again, who make Québec drag its feet. Can someone tell me please, when does one grow up in this country? Is it not so that there comes a time when every individual has to accept responsibility for his or her destiny? I know that we have inherited burdens and complexes, but is it also not our business to set things right? You would think that no one has grasped this.

I am not a defeatist nor am I a pessimist, I am simply someone who sees things as they are. Québec does not fulfill me. I am prepared to accept the good that it has to offer me, the rest I will seek elsewhere. I have no illusions that in the course of a single lifetime I could change things here. A people's mentality does not change readily, and certainly not without great effort and the passage of centuries. I have not given up. Quite the opposite, I have my cause, and my well-being takes precedence over a country that refuses to be a country.

Part One:
RESPONSES

After the appearance of my two reflective pieces in the press, a large number of individuals of all ages and backgrounds felt driven to react to my thoughts. I have had more than seventy recorded responses to what I had to say, and of these some forty appeared in the public press. These letters can be divided into three distinct groups expressing the following attitudes:

Those who detest my outlook and descend to simple name-calling; those who agree with me; and those who take an arms-length position and patronizingly pat me on the head and tell me that many had similar ideas before the Quiet Revolution,[1] and that this kind of thinking is quite normal and can lead to good things.

This set of responses suggests to me that I have touched on a sore point and that there exists in Québec society an uneasiness which it is trying—not altogether successfully—to hide. Those who would deny my perceptions as being illusory, forget that the strength of their reactions only serves to confirm the truth of what I have touched upon. Having prohibited alcohol once upon a time, we would now like to prohibit those ideas which are different from those of a silent but nevertheless suffocating majority. I am particularly interested to know the origin of this need and desire on the part of some people to convert me at any price. If, as one opinion has claimed it, I am wrong on every point, I must be alone and it would not be worth the effort to change my point of view. Surely I could not be a threat to anyone or anything. Let me be perfectly candid: I accuse those who

---

[1] This is a reference to events in the Province of Québec which led to the defeat of the Union Nationale party which had been dominant in Québec politics since 1936, and the election of a Liberal administration under Jean Lesage. One of the signal aspects of the Quiet Revolution was that it broke the hold of the Catholic Church on Québec society, especially on institutions such as education.

claim that what I say does not correspond to reality of bad and misleading faith. And there are quite a few who are in that camp. Some have even said that I am cowardly in the face of difficulties, although they could just as easily have said that to take an unpopular stance is the same as turning one's back on tough choices, thus confirming that, for some, name-calling is an antidote to that which is unpopular—as if it changes anything!

I continue to be surprised by all the things that have been said about me and my ideas. As late as August the 29TH, I still believed that the majority of Québeckers saw my point and understood what I was driving at. After all, what is so controversial about the notion that there are fools in society; that the level of our intellectual life has been declining because we have been slack and casual in our ways; and that there is no sign that this will somehow change for the better. It seems that my fault lies with having underestimated my fellow human beings' capacity for confused thinking.

For some, my dissenting point of view became an escapist way out. Why, I do not know, except that it seems that a desire to live elsewhere and to try a different way of life is typed, ingloriously, as escapism. No one tried to find out more about my reasons for thinking the way I do. They had ready-made answers for everything, and yet, it was I who was accused of choosing the easy way, I should also add that the 'faithful' among the independentists immediately conclude that anyone doubting Québec's supposed need for sovereignty must be a federalist. On this point I prefer to stand back calmly and not to be swept away by emotion. In general, I believe that keeping a healthy distance between oneself and powerful issues is a habit that we should develop. Unfortunately, we Québeckers are sadly lacking in this ability, especially when politics is involved. Surely, I need not be seen as a confirmed federalist just because I am no longer leaning on the side of sovereignty. Is the middle ground not a viable option?

But to get back to the debate. First of all, instead of showing me how or where I may be wrong, my critics plunged into hysterical and ignorant attacks upon me personally. They called me a spoiled brat making rude noises and thumbing her nose at her society. Knowing very little if anything about me they leapt to the most fantastic conclusions. For example, one individual (not untypically) concluded that I must be rich or at least from a very comfortable social mileu where life was near perfect. They concluded that they must account for my complaint about the intellectual poverty which appears to prevail here more than elsewhere. This was an easy out to explain away their own intellectual laziness. Easy excuses: "I have too many other problems"; " I do not care enough to act to stop my brain from growing soft"; "I am too busy with other things to pause even for a little bit of reflection".

My critics also tried to pinpoint all sorts of minor issues so as to marginalize my point of view and isolate me from my society. It's a pointless effort, though, because the differences that exist between them and myself are really quite insignificant. What matters is that we are all human beings with the capacity for understanding criticism and, consequently, for self-improvement. The choices are ours to make and it is useless to hide behind excuses when what really matters are the priorities to which we are committed. Except for extreme situations, each and every individual is free to make his or her choices. Is it watching hockey or reading a book; is it a soap opera or a great movie; is it a holiday of mindless sitting on a beach or is it the museum? There are intelligent alternatives for every taste and every budget, and all excuses are simply self-defeating.

It is disappointing to see my detractors concentrating on me personally rather than addressing my ideas. Are they so frustrated that they are unable to show me (and all those others who have found in me a spokeswoman for their thoughts) the error of our ways! I don't know, but I do know that asking unpopular questions in Québec is not something that is viewed with favour. They were only too happy to jump on the least trifle in order to attack my position. They criticized my writing style; they didn't like my youth nor my supposed social standing (and this without knowing anything about me); they took issue with my presumed selfishness (about which, more later), my so-called contempt, my naiveté, in short everything but the facts that I had presented and the arguments that I had advanced. Of course, it is easier to disparage an individual than to muster ideas in orderly fashion to counter arguments that are not palatable to us. It is human nature to take the easy path, but it is time for us to recognize that at a certain level of development we must act maturely and choose to make the necessary effort rather than slide off into lazy apathy.

I complain about the insults that have been hurled at me but only because these insults are proof positive that my critics are incapable of calm debate, something that would be preferable and more convincing. Actually, I am puzzled by the vehemence of these people who have accused me of being angry and of making threats, while it is I who feels a threatening anger being directed at me for my ideas. Whose problem is this anger, anyway?

There were some who questioned the relevance to Québec life of McGill University. Because I, a student among thousands of others dared to speak up, people have blamed the whole University and have questioned its ability to train the elites of Québec. I sensed personal rancour towards what I had written, and it serves to illustrate how far people will go in trying to silence those who question our society.

Obviously it is an unthinkable sacrilege that a young woman, especially a francophone woman, would dare to criticize a society which people always want to see in a perfect light. If it is normal to want to see our society as a near flawless achievement, is it not a self-deceiving act of bad faith to refuse to admit (in spite of all the daily evidence to the contrary) that we have not reached this goal and that there is room for improvement? A lot of my respondents would have preferred to see me in a role in which I would have committed myself to a battle to the end in order to achieve our objectives, and to speak only of our successes while happily closing my eyes to our shortcomings. Otherwise they would have wanted me to keep still.

They also jumped on the fact that in my young life I have not had the opportunity to travel a great deal, and while this is quite true, at the same time this does not make me some kind of a fool. If I may be allowed a grand comparison, the great German philosopher Immanuel Kant never travelled outside his native city, yet, as far as I know, no one sought to question or challenge the validity of his conclusions because he was homebound.

Some, I must say in all fairness, have praised my courage in daring to say the things that I have said. And here I must confess that my critics are right, because I did not write out of the courage of knowing what the consequences would be. Had I sensed the outcome I would, perhaps, have opted to keep quiet. I say this even though I think that more good than evil has come out of the whole affair.

Of course, there have been others who were only too willing to see me as a defeatist and a pessimist, even though what I speak of in realistic if veiled terms is no less palpable or true. I see myself as a realist: no more and no less. What I think is based on what I believe to be a clear-eyed and in no way an irrational view of circumstances. For some it is important to put much store in hope, and, if it helps them to a better life, so much the better. The only reservation that I have is that this hope is often inspired by the notion that they are duty-bound to remain in Québec or run the risk of never improving their lot. From the stand-point of simple geography this is, of course, true since it is much easier for an anglophone to quit Québec and to move away not too far and there to adapt quite easily and relatively painlessly. For a francophone to do something simi-lar and still continue to function in French he must cross the ocean, which would be asking a great deal of anyone. So, if we are stuck here it makes a lot of sense that it feels better if we believe that things will improve for us. While this attitude makes our daily lives a lot easier, it also rein-forces the notion that we must never leave Québec, and if we do, it must only be for a short time before we return. If I happened to see the situation differently I was immedi-ately labelled a defeatist. But I see myself in this, as well. I am one with a people that is friendly but distrustful of strangers. Québec is not everything, and if I suggest this it is not to attack anyone or anything, but to affirm that I have a different perception of life and that I will fight for my right to believe in it and to express it.

The word 'contempt' has appeared in the responses that some people have addressed to my articles. This is understandable if only because I have been remiss in not making a stronger point of the fact that I am, very much, part of the society which I criticize. It would have been silly of me to think that having spent my entire life in the midst of my people that I would somehow have escaped being one of them. At the same time when I am accused of seeing myself as especially cultured or intellectual, that too is a false perception. In that respect my own sense of culture is so highly set that I can only aspire to it knowing full well that it is all but unachievable. However one must continue to strive since it is possible to make little gains every day. It has also been suggested that I am "full of myself", a snob who despises others. If I give that impression it is because of my own struggle to improve myself for my own sake in the face of the intellectual slackness that surrounds me, but which is as much a part of my make-up as it is a feature of the society in which I function. That is why I am so critical: I know, only too well, the mental laziness and the preference for the easy way for which we have opted. It is not people but sloppy mental attitudes that annoy me.

It has also been stated that I am a dreamer who has a vision of utopia when I expect the factory worker to rush home to listen to a symphony, or for the average family to be discussing philosophy at breakfast. It is precisely in this assessment of my fellow citizens that I detect contempt. Naturally, we cannot expect that every single individual will be dedicated to the eternal struggle for knowledge. That, unfortunately, is the way things are. But I do believe, in spite of what I have been told, that even those people who lack certain advantages do have the capacity to improve themselves. They should see themselves as the intelligent human beings that they are. If knowledge is the domain of an intellectual elite it is because we want it to be so, and because we have chosen not to make education and learning a priority to be pursued and shared in by all members of our society.

Much more can be taught to and absorbed by our young generation which is in school up to the age of sixteen and then is forced to abandon their studies either through personal circumstances or a simple lack of motivation. Our people are not imbued by a love of learning nor by a great desire for culture. This produces disinterested students who discourage their professors who in turn and in spite of themselves become the cause of an intellectual dropping-out. Those in the position to improve our educational system seem to be disinclined to do so, preferring to keep their advantages to themselves. Those who are rich want the poor to remain ignorant since the slave who does not know that he can be free is not likely to revolt. As one study has said "We are contemptuous of those whom we would keep in ignorance and mediocrity"[1]. It is precisely this contempt that lurked behind many of the letters that I received which, all the while, attempted to place this very attitude at my doorstep. Quite the contrary, I deplore the fact that no one has taken the trouble in a would-be country, especially one that it is struggling to affirm itself, to insist that we need people who are well-educated and capable of thinking for themselves. Education and culture are tools of self-understanding, but when I propose them not just as desirable goals but as fundamental objectives for our society I am told

---

[1] Association québecoise des professeurs de français, Le Livre noir, Editions du Jour, p.17

that I am being contemptuous. It is strange reasoning, indeed, which interprets an attempt to arouse people to self-awareness as an expression of contempt. I think that I've heard just about enough! The well-intentioned seem to want me to leave people alone since, apparently, they have neither the time nor the energy to think about their situation.

There is a gap between those who have the power (by which we should understand, money) and most of the know-how (although the two could quite easily be kept separate), and the rest of the population immersed in its lassitude and its indifference. I would like to rouse the people from their torpor, and for this I am showered with brickbats. Let it be perfectly clear, I do not see myself as some kind of a saviour, but I would like people to recognize that those who accuse others of arrogance are the ones who are usually guilty of contempt for their fellow-citizens. After all it is in their interest to defend their position and their status, and is it not true that the best defense is an attack?

I have been dealing with ideas relating to culture, knowledge and learning. If I have not defined these terms precisely it is because I am still thinking them through, a process which does not make them any less valid. Defined or not, some have done my defining for me by analysing what I have outlined in my articles. They have concluded that my idea of culture is that of a purist and an elitist, and that I believe that culture is a kind of straightforward question and answer thing. But I have never argued that culture is an accumulation of raw data. Rather, my point has been that we have to start with raw data which must be digested and thought about in an open-minded fashion. Culture is not a pile of facts and figures, but it is from such an accumulation that it frequently derives. Nor do I see it so much as a monolithic structure, but rather as a field of knowledge encompassing everything and anything. I do not limit myself to literature or to the arts exclusively; I would simply like to have as much knowledge as possible. That is why I continue to believe that self-improvement consists of reaching for this ideal, even if it is unattainable. Those who have labelled me a purist have also decided that I despise American movies and the whole of American culture. Nothing could be farther from the truth. The Americans, like everybody else, have their strong points, and if we want to confine the debate by speaking only of their frivolous movies all of which resemble one another, let us at least admit that they are usually entertaining. It is all very good and fine to be always engaged in the serious pursuit of culture, but there must also be a time and a place to relax. I am not against entertainment. Only, it must not become a way of life.

I have also been accused of confusing education with culture. Of course they have been associated in my discussion, and it is difficult to keep them absolutely separate, but I do not see them as being synonymous. Of course there are those who are educated without being cultured and vice versa, but in a society such as ours where neither one is particularly valued or respected, I believe that it should be the function of education to promote cultural values and the pursuit of knowledge. The schoolroom cannot teach everything, but it should be encouraged (and expected) to give its students the desire to explore beyond its walls. The school should tantalize the student with a foretaste of that which is possible in a wider sense. Some of this, of course, does take place, but on such a modest scale that it's laughable. Culture is not education, but education opens the road to culture.

Another kind of criticism which I had to face had to do with my declared intention to spoil my ballot in the forthcoming election thus denying my vote to Mr. Jacques Parizeau because he had promised to eliminate fees for those having to repeat failed courses at the CEGEP level. This was seen as not a particularly profound piece of political action or political reasoning. I don't really care. At least I took a stand in the face of a political party that is not any more perfect than the others. Most people—regrettably—vote without thinking. This was not going to be my case, and I accept all responsibility for my decision. I could not, in conscience, vote for a political party that was prepared to encourage laziness and failure. There was no need for any kind of profound political analysis of a blatantly stupid electoral promise. I know from personal experience that minimal effort and attention is all that is required to pass in most CEGEP courses. Most voters would not even pause to think about this, nor for that matter are they very familiar with the process at college, but I know how it works and I could not let such a piece of stupidity go unchallenged.

As far as being selfish, a sentiment of which I am supposed to be guilty, I have no difficulty with it. What is selfishness to some is, to my mind, looking after oneself first. I am not impressed with those who claim to be purely altruistic in their actions. If we give to those who are poor, or if we help others in some way, let us remember that we do it because it is satisfying to us. If an individual is devoted to his or her country it is because it produces a sense of wellbeing and not because we lose ourselves in the collectivity. We have all heard it said that a child is selfish because it expects others to take care of all its needs. Well, an adult is very similar except that adults have different needs and pleasures, and are more subtle in the ways in which they seek to be gratified. It seems to me that women have always wanted to save the world, and since, latterly, they have learnt to think and speak about themselves without feeling guilty about it, I think that it is backward-looking to deny me the right to express myself on these points.

My so-called selfishness has been identified with my refusal to immerse myself in the body politic of Québec, something that is seen as an unacceptable stance. I am intended to understand by all this that, for the common good, I should melt happily and silently into the mass of my people. But what is this mass? A sleepy people with malfunctioning institutions and insignificant problems of which we talk all the time without attacking the real issues of our lives. There were conflicting different messages: some thought that I was wrong-headed to be so individualistic while others deplored the fact that Québeckers lacked individualism. So, what is it to be?

I have also read that I am an example of a monstrous social disaffiliation, an opinion at which people arrived because they discerned that I no longer have faith in our dear Québecois political system. Naturally, I must be wrong in this sentiment, for is it not an **ABSOLUTE MUST** to fight for your country, to wallow in that which is politically correct, or, failing that at least to be quiet and pretend not to exist. No one pauses, not even for a second, to ask the all-important question: Are we right in believing in the political maturity of Québec? Do we really need sovereignty? Do we need sovereignty **NOW?** And if so, why? Does political action really achieve anything? Are there not a thousand little things, concrete things, that would really improve the lives of ordinary people, and are these not more important than sovereignty which will only change the label on Québec? I would like to believe in the independence of Québec. I would also like to have good and solid and rational reasons to believe in it. The problem is that for most Québeckers, independence is someone else's dream for which, only too frequently, they have no explanation. Perhaps, that in itself is not so bad or so wrong, but taking account of our financial difficulties and realizing that political uncertainty may deprive us of the few remaining luxuries that we can still afford, ideals and dreams become readily expendable. An individual by himself or herself in the polling booth feels terribly lonely, and that is quite understandable. If only he or she had weighed the political pros and cons and then had decided to make sacrifices then he or she would be armed with the facts of that decision and would feel confident in that booth.

The choice whether to stay in Canada or not has, generally speaking, not had the benefit of extended reflection. Is it a sense of security; the Rocky Mountains; the pension? We don't go much further than that. There are many reasons for this kind of political superficiality, but it can all be summarized by saying that it is mainly due to laziness and the desire of politicians and interest groups to obscure the facts because it serves their purposes. For example, we have talked for a long time about the Canadian constitution, but only a tiny minority felt sufficiently concerned about the problem to find out for themselves what it was all about. Yet much has been written on the subject. Another example, all the numerous studies on the real cost of sovereignty which are not being released or which were carried out by people who are very far from being neutral on the subject. One way or another, nobody seems to have all the facts, and therefore nobody is in the position to make an informed decision.

We are told that the independence of a people is achieved by political action of the heart and guts. That may be true, but generally a country gains its independence as a result of a grave crisis or upheaval. What influences and determines momentous action is not just optimism but a sense of desperate and necessary urgency. Here, we have neither famine nor war, nor for that matter an oppressive regime despite what some sovereigntists would have us believe. This is what causes a divided mind in the people. Because there is no emergency there will not be some glorious action leading to the 'liberation of Québec'. And it is for this reason, a lack of emotional and spiritual drive, that sovereignty must be achieved through reason.

I have also been typed as a stingy person who studies here only because of the cost of tuition which happens to be lower than in other places. The complaints have been loud, and I have been accused of intolerable behaviour because I am supposed to be abusing the educational system. This is a laughable piece of hypocrisy. Everyone— and I repeat it again, everyone is guilty of some form of abuse against the system. Anyone who has bought the smallest item on the black market; anyone who has not declared all their income; anyone who has claimed more than warranted on an insurance loss; all of these, in one way or another, abuse the system. So what is all this pious hypocrisy about? Every one would like to get full value for their money or their efforts, and even the most scrupulous individual finds it hard to resist getting a little bit more than what they are entitled to provided that they are safe from being discovered. It is pointless to get emotional about this, since it simply proves our blindness when faced with reality, be that our reality or that of our neighbours.

Furthermore, many people only see the reality by which they are confronted. If they are specialists in anything, their reality is coloured by that in which they are knowledgeable. This narrowness of vision impairs their critical sense. Thus a student in literature when referring to a passage in my first article where I compared certain Québecois attitudes to those prevalent in the Middle Ages, tried to correct me, saying that in the Middle Ages acts of courage were inspired by the sentiment of courtly love. I had meant quite the opposite in my remarks, observing as I did that attempts at personal growth and development were usually suffocated by the habits and practices of the Middle Ages. To see the Middle Ages in the narrow set of terms suggested by notions of courtly love is as wrong as it would be for a future historian to interpret our times in terms of the Harlequin romance and not on the basis of the every day realities lived by the people. Courtly love: the operative word is courtly which conjures up the privileged existence of courts and royal favour. I am quite sure that the ordinary folk of the Middle Ages lived lives which were very far, indeed, from any kind of courtly connection. Real life is not literature, and daily reality is made up of a multiplicity of factors and not of a single and narrowly-defined perspective.

Be that as it may, it is worth noting that the majority of reactions that disagreed with me consisted of personal insults, small-minded insinuations and gratuitous observations. It seems to me that disagreement inevitably leads to disagreeable confrontation. Having freed ourselves of our image of good little Catholics, polite and quiet, it is time that we taught ourselves the art of reasonable debate. Different points of view and challenging the givens of life can lead to great things provided we do not sweep them away. Maybe this is another sign of the complex imposed upon us by the Church (with our consent, of course, even if we may not have been aware of it); namely, that when one is not certain of one's opinions one is reluctant to question them. But question we must, because rational discussion will lead us farther than a random stabbing in the dark.

Another important point. We appear to be living in a period of the politically correct. Thus, most of the letters sent to the papers about my articles fell in with what can be seen as a correct position: An optimistic outlook; a belief in Québec; in short everything that should form the platform of the pre-referendum campaign. However, in the letters that came to me privately, there was very little of this kind of posturing, which tells me that it is much easier to side with the majority—especially in public! All of this does not move me to think in terms of changing my position. I am simply waiting for proof positive that I am wrong. I want it proved to me with facts and not with sentiments that I do not share and cannot force upon myself. Somehow I doubt that this will happen.

There is a surprising dimension to all of this. The notion of **COUNTRY** writ large has emerged, and all of a sudden people are defining themselves in terms of the geographical location where they were born. I am told that if I leave I will go to a country that can never be mine. But what is a country? Is Québec a country? I am not convinced by the 40% who supposedly want independence, a percentage of the population that fluctuates up and down unceasingly. I am not looking for a country. I find the idea too abstract and too confusing. What I want is a milieu which is as vast and open as possible. I do not deny that Québec will always remain my birthplace, but I want to distance myself somewhat from this awareness, especially since it is important not to underestimate a determined person's ability to adapt to new situations. As far as I know we are not nailed to our native soil, and there is nothing to keep us confined to it other than the opinions of fellow-citizens which seek to limit the scope of our possibilities.

I have also been reproached for generalizing too much thus serving to set the cat among the pigeons, as it were. I can understand the feelings of those who are particularly exercised by those unflattering generalizations which tend to include them. But the same people are pleased and proud when an athlete from Québec scores an olympic success. Then this athlete is no longer an individual who has won in their sport but becomes all of Québec. Each and every spectator in their living room is filled with pride just as if it is they who had suffered the injuries and endured the privations of the rigours of training. No one objects, then, when the awards and medals are presented to the pride and glory of Québec. So, instead of getting angry at what I have to say with my generalizations, it would be better to pause and think for a while. The critical sensibility to which we should all aspire should include the ability to judge oneself. This might lead to a certain kind of clear mindedness. It matters little that if after having recognized our weaknesses we tolerate them. The important thing is to have acknowledged their existence. There is no place for false pride in these circumstances.

Turning now to personal interviews, I was surprised that my interviewers seemed not to know what questions to ask me. There was some concern whether my friends thought as I do. Of course some share my views while others do not. The journalists with whom I spoke—and, I suspect, their audience—were apprehensive about a possible revolt of the younger generation. A revolt the advent of which they had altogether missed. If there is a revolt brewing I know nothing of it. If I claim that I am not alone in thinking as I do it is not because there is an organized group out there ready to throw bombs, but because I know and sense that there are many others, and not necessarily of my age group, who think as I do.

It seems that many readers were reminded of their own youth, although they were likely to pity me or to type me as a whiner and complainer. They, of course, were different when they were my age... This is an easy way out of an argument, stressing my youth and writing my message off as due to the existential crisis of passing out of adolescence into young adulthood. Any excuse will do to discredit the young who talk too much. But the truth is that I have had letters both for and against my outlook from a wide range of people from seventeen to eighty-six., which is to say that I touched many age groups out there, and they were not all living through the same identity crisis which I was supposedly experiencing.

Perhaps, given a little more time, my charming critics would have found an explanation for the state of mind of my older sympathisers. I know this for a fact since I myself had the distinct pleasure of being psycho-analyzed at a distance by perfect strangers! If I sound angry, they say, it must be because I am frustrated in my love life. Clearly, I crave so much for Québec to be perfect that when I see that it is imperfect, I want to punish it by spitting upon and leaving it in disgust. Thus everything is explained. I am scatterbrained and irrational and consumed by vengefulness, and there is no need to pay any attention to me. If this diagnosis reassures my worthy analyst, so much the better. He is not alone in being dismissive of my anger. I make no apologies for being angry. I wanted, in the best possible context, to wake up a few people. I don't know if I achieved it, but I am certain of the fact that people read what I had to say. It is also likely that the anger attributed to me was not mine alone, but that it was seized upon by those who felt particularly attacked by my point of view. I may be discouraged by certain aspects of Québec, as well as by things about the human race in general, but I have neither the time nor the energy to be totally preoccupied with this.

Let us bear in mind that there are those who have reached the same conclusions as I have, but then they have gone on to point out that there are two possible ways of addressing the problem: to adopt my attitude which is seen as defeatist, or to face up to it proudly. Of course it is very noble to be proud of one's country as I have been told, but what of the lack of intellectual stimulus? What are we to make of it, and what is there of which we should be be proud? On this point they are silent. There are also those who have offered their optimism as a choice to which one can subscribe as much as the notion of pride proposed by others. While I don't want to reject these options categorically, it seems to me that being realistic is still the best path to follow if only because blind optimism obscures the reality, and until I have seen proof to the contrary I will continue to be a realist.

I have also been reminded of the achievements of

Québec: students who supposedly perform better than in the rest of Canada; of technological breakthroughs, and God knows what else. My critics felt that I had not given this element fair play. But I do not see how some or even many achievements change the large reality of the majority. If we have successful researchers, artists or athletes, so much the better. If our students excel in certain subjects, so much the better . I am concerned, though,that here again it is the easy way out, insisting that we cannot be that hopeless since there are those who appear to be be even worse than we are. What does that change?

The people of Québec must never become complacent because they may be better than some others. They should measure themselves against their own standards, as should all of us individually. It is important not to say, "I want to be better than so and so", but to encourage oneself to improve, since that is what really matters. While we feel proud when this or that study reveals that our students have performed three or five percent better than other little Canadians in some test, we tend to forget all those other times when we have not fared so well or, even worse, did not even place in the competition. If, once in a while, Québec proves to be better, there are also times when it is worse, so that this kind of comparison does not serve to raise us above criticism or reproach. For example: the Research Council on Science and Technology has recently submitted a report to the Government in which it complains about the quality of teaching in the Sciences in Québec as compared to other territories. The report also talks about the levelling downwards that is widespread, and also of the lack of stimulus and encouragement for the better students. Yet our pseudo excellence was cited to me frequently in letters of reaction to my opinions as if there were no difficulties or problems to contend with. It may be that this came from those who claimed to have taken the path of optimism, although it would seem that they were practising optimism as a kind of comforting and blinding religion. It is quite possible to see only the good side of everything and without considering all the facts, something that has been recommended to me when praising various Québec successes. Only, I am afraid that this will lead us to a false sense of well-being if we keep ignoring our weaknesses because we choose not to look at them. Moreover how will we be able to overcome them?

Looking back now I am struck by all sorts of unbelievable things that have been said to me. Statements such as: "Certainly, our system of education has its weak points, but…". Always this qualification, always this "Certainly… but…". It is as if these words were not meant to say anything, as if they have lost their ability to make a statement that people can understand. But these words are also a symbol of the extent of our cynicism and of our indifference. A simple sentence introducing a paragraph to explain why I am an imbecile tells me everything. It betrays to me without being aware of it, that people have accepted the terrible failures that are taking place in many Québec classrooms (and in other places too, perhaps). How can we be so accepting and so complacent about the situation? How can we say "certainly… but…" and then go on to other things? Even the word flaws is an euphemism chosen with care and cunning to hide the true state of affairs which happens to be far more serious than the word flaws indicates.

As far as the human element is concerned, I was told rather pointedly, that it must supercede the cultural and the intellectual, although, this strikes me as a pretty feeble argument. I was also told that culture in the broadest sense of the word was not everything, and that generosity of the spirit and tolerance of the values of others were the basis of true knowledge. But I feel that sacrificing one in favour of the other of these two considerations denies the fundamentally human search for balance and equilibrium in all things. Of course one can be happy without having studied anything, without having travelled, and without knowing very much. And maybe that is the best way, but why settle for so little when the human spirit has the potential to soar to unknown heights? And such aspirations take nothing away from our "humanity". To see these two sides of human experience as opposed to one another is to deny the very nature of being.

There is a tendency on the part of many people to see things only in terms of white and black. Thus, the choice for them is between optimism and pessimism without any allowance for realism which lies between the two extremes. For them there is no widened scope of perception. We have enough problems as it is with which we have to cope , they say, without getting into intellectual debates. It is distracting to argue about culture when there are pressing issues such as the environment, women's place in society, the role of minorities and the unequal distribution of wealth, all of which are problems that afflict our society. Here again, there is a refusal to entertain the possibility that we may be confronted by a variety of issues simultaneouly, granted that some will be more urgent than others. The snag in this kind of reasoning is that social problems become a kind of barrier which prevents us from going beyond the immediate. They become an excuse even though we are not doing much to address them. And then, of course, it is possible that we will never solve these social problems: something over which our beautiful system can agonize... But I believe that solutions are entirely possible, and that the answer lies in education and the communication of knowledge. It is not a miraculous way out (since miracles, in spite of what we have been told, do not occur) but it will help us in various ways to advance in our thinking and our discussions. Under the guise of urgent needs elsewhere we have shrugged off knowledge; under the guise of seeking quick and immediate resolution of issues we have sacrificed the prospect of considered and lasting solutions of our problems.

Often when I am reproached for the superficiality of my views, people choose not to explain their own position believing it to be so obviously right, intelligent and self-evident that I must be stupid not to see it myself. Their "do not expect me to explain everything to you" attitude is, of course, more facile than the supposed superficialities of which they accuse me. After all it is much easier not to have to defend one's ideas than to have to rack one's brains for proof in their defence. They are determined, almost pathologically, to avoid a challenge to their ideas at any cost. I think that if these people refuse to defend their point of view, we are entitled to doubt the validity of that which they believe and propose.

I have also been advised to breathe through the nose, to smoke a joint, to read André Malraux (or others), and to listen to the songs of Richard Desjardins... I don't know what that will do for me. I like the songs of Desjardins, but that doesn't change my sense of reality. Will one song or one book suddenly enlighten me and make me see the error of my ways? That is a gentle way to let me know that my ideas are superficial, and although others have been more brutally direct, I am still waiting for them to come up with concrete proof. Smoke a joint?

Why? Because it relaxes you? Yes, if I only had time to relax, perhaps to change my ideas about Québec society (since that seems to be the real objective of this advice). This is all too ridiculous. Breathe through my nose! Could it be that I am being told to shut up because what I say is disturbing? All of it seems to suggest that they will say anything so as to spare themselves the pain of thinking. I find all this very doubtful...

I have also been congratulated for having expressed my ideas and for being articulate. Of course, compliments are always nice, but I have the feeling that there was an element of condescension in this, as if someone my age should not really have ideas or be able to express them effectively in writing. And it is I who is accused of being condescending!

In the same spirit, some took pleasure in addressing me as a young adult to whom they would explain the ways of the world, reinforcing their ideas with bargain-basement philosophic platitudes, for after all was I not too young to have intelligent ideas, and was I not too young to touch on topics which are taboo? But that's alright. What I cannot stomach is the fact that I am reproached for a lack of depth in my arguments which, I know cannot appeal to everyone and which need maturing, while all along my critics are guilty of pedantry and the misuse of long words in their attempt to silence me. They have even quoted snippets from a popular song in an attempt to persuade me to change my mind. The problem, though, is not that I want to abandon that which I love, I simply do not want to stagnate. And abandon is a heavy word. To want to go somewhere else is not to abandon. I know from experience that you can continue to relate to things even at a distance. Poetry is one thing, but the reality of life is something else. In any case, a borrowing from a popular song does not make a very convincing argument. For every such quotation I can respond with one of my own choice, and nothing will be resolved by this exchange. By the way, is this another manifestation of our inferiority complex, this tendency to use the words of someone else rather than rely on our own? Naturally, we can borrow from others when what they say corresponds exactly to what we are trying to convey, but if this practice becomes wholesale one cannot help but wonder. It is noteworthy that the majority of those who wrote to the papers tried very hard to work into their arguments the names of great authors or quotations from their writings. Could it be that they were trying to show their immense learning, or could it be that they did not think that their own ideas and words were as weighty as those of others? Little by little, and almost imperceptibly, we seem to be losing our language and with it a little bit of ourselves.

On the other side of this debate, there were those who told me that what I had expressed had been on their minds for a long time, which is to say that I did not start anything but simply gave voice to what others had been thinking. However, this was akin to a crime for some even though others agreed with me. I think that it is essential to question things so that people are shaken out of their customary torpor, even if the status quo can be a comfortable state of mind. I am sure that there are those who would have preferred for me to have complained unheard in my little cor-

ner. But that would not have changed the fact that there are
some people who think, and it is futile to try to squelch
them in the belief that "what we do not know cannot hurt
us". Or should this phrase be the motto of the future country *cum* utopia of Québec?

Part Two

"In every Québecker there dozes a man
who pretends that he is awake even though
he doesn't lift a finger.
I claim that he is asleep."
(Gilles Vigneault)

Politics

IN POLITICS, LIES ARE KING. NOT ONLY IS IT THAT politicians never answer a question directly, but people, somehow, seem to prefer to be lied-to brazenly. The truth is too black for them to want to see it. But ignoring it will not make our problems go away, and while I lack the credentials to provide all the answers, I prefer to be in touch with the real world rather than pretend to be aware. Let's be consistent in our analysis of the situation. The primary focus of the last election campaign was on job creation, and while I am not absolutely sure that is what the people voted for, it was what the politicians concentrated on. It was a question of who would create more jobs regardless of the means. But is this proposition an illusion? In order to create jobs the government has to invest funds which it has to take from the taxpayer who then is deprived of this disposable income. If consumer spending is affected in this manner, production stagnates and jobs are lost. It's a case of robbing one to pay the other. Of course there are subtleties in the way in which this can be done, and I suppose, it is possible to take a little bit from each and every one and then redistribute it as jobs and financial assistance, but it all comes down to the same thing, and we are still beset by the same problems. Most political solutions are of this nature, not so much a sleight-of-hand, but really a very short-term remedy. In addition, there is no proof that even with improved conditions and the best of intentions it will be possible to increase the number of jobs. The labour market is saturated, and in order to achieve prosperity we have to accept the notion of progress which means the elimination of some jobs or the loss of their value. It is also probable that the situation will get even worse although no one seems inclined to confront the politicians with this prospect. Why?

Because people prefer to be lied to. It is more reassuring to believe that something can still be done. The same is true of the deficit and our social programmes. The politician who tells us that the problem is not too grave and that things can be fixed without too many painful sacrifices is sure to win in the popularity stakes, and that is all that counts.

DEMOCRACY

How are we to know if during an election we have made the right choice? It seems to me that it is impossible to differentiate between truth and lies; how is it possible when we do not have access to documents or to accurate forecasts, and when, moreover, we lack the knowledge to verify the accuracy of our conclusions. We vote without proper knowledge even if we have listened to the debates and read the newspapers. How can we be certain of the problems and their place in the political scheme of things. In a time of crisis we vote for the one who appears to be most likely to solve our problems quickly, the one, that is, who tells us what we want to hear. This year the people want to pay less taxes, they want jobs, and they don't want cuts in our social programmes. But in reality all that can be done is to move the taxes around a bit by burying them in the cost of things; take jobs away here and give them somewhere else; and preserve the universality of our social programmes a little longer until the structure breaks, because everyone knows that things cannot go on much longer because the expectations of our social programmes are not realistic. The days of the all-giving State are finished, and with it the days of social security for all. It's over.

While waiting we vote, but for whom? Is it really

important? It doesn't matter what a party holds dear, whoever becomes prime minister won't have much room to manoeuvre. He may be able to give us the semblance of a solution, and he may even be liked for a little while, or he may choose to tell the truth, to down-size, to cut here and there where it is deemed necessary and thus provoke a great revulsion in the electorate.

So, I have asked myself: Why should I vote? In the name of democracy? Since nothing changes—the differences between political parties is just smoke in our eyes, since once elected they must make do with what little they have which leaves them with few options—what is the point of this famous democracy? We do not choose the best solutions, we choose a leader, whoever that may be, who will have very little freedom. And if democracy is just a beautiful dream, was Communism also not a dream which burst like a soap bubble? The Russians are paying dearly for that dream, and it may very well be that we are on the verge of having to pay for ours even though we—as Westerners—may try to resist it to the bitter end.

I am also not impressed by those who would take the easy way and tell me that communism, as such, was not viable, because the communism that was put in place was not the communism of Marx, although that is not important because lots of people believed in it just as many of us believe in our system. Marx said that communism would come after a capitalist phase during which great riches would be amassed. Capitalism would end in a collapse due to this emphasis on the accumulation of wealth which would be followed by a period of socialism which, in turn, would lead into communism. The communist countries of our time did not go through a period of capitalism with its amassing of wealth which may account in part for their failure. They ignored the need to amass wealth before distributing it. Our own experience—and Marx did not anticipate it—allowed us to avoid the collapse of capitalism (the New Deal in the States was one such preventive measure). However, how long can we continue to avoid it? And will socialism emerge as the solution? I do not think so, and nothing at present leads me to believe in it.

THE REFERENDUM

When people go around saying "it is not going well" they are referring to everyday things, to the shortage of money and to rising prices. As a solution we are offered high-sounding alternatives: on the one hand, independence; on the other hand, "change", a rejection of the "status quo" . And it matters little what we understand by these terms. It's very nice, but will any one of these "solutions" really solve our problems? The problems of those who do not have enough to eat, of those who leave school too early to go to work, of those who at the age of forty or fifty lose their jobs and cannot find other employment?

Are they not attempting—still—to conceal the truth from us? Are we not being led to be shorn like sheep? In electing Jacques Parizeau last September, Québeckers accepted the cost of having yet another referendum—the second in the last fifteen years—on independence. Everyone knows that a public sounding of such magnitude is an extremely costly thing. So, why do it?

The facts are these. We had a referendum in 1980 and the majority decision was to stay in Canada. However this majority appears to have lost the referendum since here we are, fifteen years later, ready to hold another referendum without any regard for the earlier decision. We could argue that things have changed in the last fifteen years, and that there has been massive change in Québec society. One could defend this notion of an evolving society, but it does not change the complexion of things a great deal. Our society today is not that much different from that of 1980. Certainly, there are areas which have undergone great change, but these elements by themselves do not make up our society. There are many more immigrants now among us who have the right to vote, and the majority of them will vote against sovereignty not because they are "against us" but because many of them were welcomed warmly and helped by the anglophone community while, not infrequently, being rejected by the francophones. For this we have only ourselves to blame. The population, also, is aging, and even if the young generation, by and large, favours sovereignty, their numbers are not large enough to affect significantly the final outcome.

We have to look elsewhere in order to have a change in our society that would have an effect on the referendum. I am referring to those who were able to vote in 1980, and of whom at least twenty percent must change their mind in favour of sovereignty. This is wildly optimistic since it presupposes that these people recognize that they made a mistake in 1980; that the reasons for voting the way they did in 1980 no longer hold true for them; and that they are now motivated to correct their earlier mistake. This would be nice, but it is naive to think that a fifth of the population erred so seriously in 1980 that they could be persuaded to reverse themselves on a question so charged with consequence as the proposed sovereignty of Québec. It becomes obvious therefore that the majority of Québeckers will still vote "No" in the next referendum.

There is another question in all this. If the majority decision of fifteen years ago carries no weight with us today and is discounted, how can anyone insist that, by the same token, a majority decision in favour of sovereignty today would somehow have validity? Where will this lead us if we dismiss a majority decision simply because it did not provide us with a hoped for result? René Levesque had it in his mind to hold several referenda if the first one came out against the desired result. I have even been told that it will be worth our while to keep on having referenda so long as there is at least one believer in sovereignty out there. How can any one be so lacking in seriousness as to propose throwing millions out of the window?

We can easily understand that politicians are in this for the advantages that it will bring to them, but they should also remember that they are where they are in order to carry out the public's will, or, at least, to respect it. Thus, to keep asking at great cost the same question about independence when only a minority favours the idea is a pure and simple waste of public funds. Even worse, it proves that some politicians are completely out of touch with reality, and that they are, moreover, intellectually dishonest. I am speaking here of politicians, but they are not alone in profiting from this eternally ongoing debate. It is frequently the case that the wealthy are the ones who profit from the economic and political uncertainty of a society. While we are engaged in speech-making on the future of the nation we forget that there are others who do not have enough to eat, and still others who do away with themselves rather than live in a world such as ours. The debate about independence may have had its origins with the people, but it has now become the preserve of a certain elite.

We do not ask the people for their opinion, we simply ask them to vote for independence. It is only a question of time and persistence, the politicians think. If we ask the question often enough, eventually, just like a bored daddy beset by an insistent child, the public will give us the "yes" that we want. It is almost as if we held two or three elections at the same time and then chose the result that most favoured us. Isn't democracy lovely?

I want to make it perfectly clear that I am in favour of raising questions and believe them to be beneficial. But I also believe that sovereignty, when it comes, will not be the product of a minority (and let's be truthful here and call things by their name) convincing the others. Sovereignty must come from a fundamental and all-encompassing movement of society and not from intellectuals and eternal dreamers. It must be a life or death situation for a people. The morose contentment in which we are sunk does not lend itself to that.

Why make sacrifices for a change of labels which will change nothing in the concrete realities of our lives? That is what people are really thinking, and I cannot blame them. Taking the easy way may not be the most fortunate alternative, but it is entirely human.

By remaining more or less tacitly open to the idea of a referendum, Québeckers have chosen to sit on the fence (again !), and to keep all options open. One wonders how long we can continue to do this without getting hurt, just as it is necessary to ask how much each one of us wants to invest in a referendum which we all know in advance will be lost. The Parti Québecois was elected by too slim a margin to give real encouragement to fierce sovereigntists. It is also high time to squelch the idea that the government spends "its" money. It spends the money that it takes out of our pockets: the referendum will be paid for by our money. Do we really want that? If each one of us was asked to contribute X dollars for the cost of running the referendum with a clear indication of where that money was going there would be no referendum. For the moment we prefer to think that what we do not know does not hurt us. Sure, we say, there is a bit of my money in this, but what the hell . . . Are there really that many people who have money to give for lost causes, especially when these may be causes in which they do not believe?

Independence can only come when each citizen takes his responsibility seriously. When each and every one of us will be prepared to assign a part of his or her income to the project of sovereignty, and when we recognize that the country of Québec cannot come about without sacrifices. Then we can talk of the public's wish for sovereignty but not before. Unfortunately, clear thinking frightens people.

The difference between 1980 and now is that then there was René Levesque who roused our passions. It was easy to delude oneself about winning the referendum; a crowd does not realize that it is alone. Today, there is no delirious crowd and no great "Chief" to move mountains (or at least to try). The numbers are about the same, 60/40, but today we are under no illusion. Not only is there nothing that threatens us, but there is also no popular ground-swell.

In 1980 René Levesque demonstrated his keen sense of marketing when he said "until the next time". Where would the debate be today had he not said "until the next time"?

Well, we have arrived at this "next time", and Jacques Parizeau and his team are trying to cover their rear by having us vote on a law of the National Assembly and not on an absolutely clear question as has been proposed by Prime Minister Chrétien: "Do you want, yes or no, for Québec to separate from Canada?" It is not hard to see why he is asking this question. He is sure that because of our fear of definite commitments he will win his bet. Similarly, by avoiding a direct and candid question, the Parti Québecois is keeping a back door open for an escape. If (and can anyone doubt the outcome?) the majority votes "no", the Parti Québecois can pretend that it was not a rejection of independence but only of the law. In a few years they will be back again. This is a good tactic from the point of view of a political party determined to achieve its ends, but for our society it is just more of this going around in circles.

We should also ask ourselves if this so-called desire for independence is not a new way to put the blame for our ills on someone else, in this case the federal government. But once sovereignty is achieved (let's just imagine it), and the federal government is out of the picture, whom will we blame for the problems of the world? It's easy. First we'll blame the political party that led us into independence. And who after that? There will always be a scapegoat, and we will do our utmost to avoid taking personal responsiblity for our situation.

Committed sovereigntists admit that their solution is not a panacea. It will not solve all our problems, but, they contend, it will give us the means to fix certain things. But it will not solve intellectual problems, and it will not give us the will to face those problems either. I don't think that it will solve anything. It has even been suggested that independence will change our mentality. I doubt it. The dictionary defines mentality as the sum total of the beliefs and habits that inform and order the thought of a collectivity, and it is something that the members of the collectivity subscribe to and have in common. And since humans, in spite of themselves, do not change quickly or easily, it is difficult to discern what independence can possibly do to change our mentality.

It is even believed that everything will be set right when Québeckers feel confident in themselves, and that this confidence will come with independence. It is possible that confidence will solve our problems, but I see nothing that guarantees that independence will give us confidence. One thing is certain, nothing is automatic. We have let our confidence go by the board for two hundred years, and it will not be a few months or a few years that will suffice to regain it.

Problems are like microbes. We find a remedy for them and they mutate and come back even stronger. For example, in 1960 René Levesque, elected for the first time, deplored the fact that too many youths were dropping out of school at fifteen due to a lack of accessible university places. He proposed various ways and means to remedy the situation and to assist those who wanted to continue with their education. According to him, the provincial government should stop waiting on Ottawa and act on its own. Here we are thirty-five years later and the high drop-out rate has replaced limited access as the issue. The problem which we thought had been solved has reappeared under a different guise. They can go to school but they don't want to because they have chosen to emphasise other priorities. What has happened is that the change which was necessary in 1960 and is still necessary is more profound than the remedy suggested by a political solution. The problem is one of our ideas about education, of our lack of motivation, and of the value we place on knowledge. If nobody recognizes the problem and no one wants to hear about it, how can we hope to solve it? The drop-out rate or the lack of adequate or sufficient education (university not being necessarily the solution) are only examples of recurring problems. There are others which are even more serious. A general awareness and concern would be much more effective than all the laws and measures of the government which, even if they have a short-term benefit, do not change anything fundamentally in the long run.

To avoid further misunderstanding and at the risk of not being believed, I would like to share my political vision. I do this because it is surprising how many people have read me superficially and have not reached beyond the surface of what I have been trying to say. I am convinced that, as a people, Québeckers have to take their lives into their own hands, and this not as "old" and "pure" Québeckers— which is to say white and French-speaking—but as Québeckers to be defined in a way yet to be determined. It is to be expected that in the normal course of events and having survived the trials and tribulations of this passage the ensemble of our people will move together towards independence, and that each individual will have undergone their own process leading to the same point. A regular process of evolution should have made us citizens of a new country in 1980. If we faltered it was because we chose to. Of course there was the campaign of fear and blackmail of Pierre Elliot Trudeau, but it is we who let ourselves be influenced by these fears. A genuine conviction should not fold in the face of hypothetical threats.

This having been said, two considerations remain to be addressed. Either our social development has stopped in adolescence, or we are slower in this process than other countries that have become independent, and our independence will come sooner or later. Given the circumstances we should opt for the first possibility: there is no desperate need or oppressive situation that urges our evolution along, nor is there a pressing requirement that we become complete in ourselves. Maybe what we are experiencing is the residue of our Christian background which makes us self-effacing and accepting. There is nothing to be done about it except to let time do its work, if such is our destiny. In the mean time let us concentrate on real problems hoping that the situation will clear up.

I am no longer a committed sovereigntist, rather I am a sovereigntist who has become discouraged with sovereignty. The absence of a charismatic leader who is also a crowd-pleasing speaker is surely one of the reasons why we have become lackadaisical, although that should not matter greatly since if a leader can change our attitude as easily as all that then it shows that our beliefs are superficially based.

There has been a lot of talk about how much time Mr. Parizeau has at his disposal to convince people that his option is right for Québec. The idea of having to "convince" is itself an annoyance. Neither Mr. Parizeau nor anyone else should be trying to convince people. We are not dealing with children who have to be convinced to get dressed but with people who are being asked to decide about the future of a country. This is a decision that does not spring up in a couple of months but should develop out of the experience of a life time. If the political parties which are presently locked in a struggle believe that they have to convince people, they will waste a lot of time and money. Those who are on the "yes" side as much as those who are opposed have their own reasons for their convictions, and in politics just as in matters of religion, one cannot force people to change their point of view. If one tries to convince the undecided, that too is offensive since being undecided is also a position and does not necessarily mean uncertainty or hesitation.

It is impossible to convince people for a very simple reason: for every argument that one presents the other side can counter with an equally convincing but opposite point. All depends on the point of view that has been adopted. Thus there are two ways of viewing the fact that Québeckers want (supposedly) a second referendum in a period of fifteen years. On the one hand one can say that the people of Québec have matured and gained in self-confidence very quickly when it was thought that the defeat of 1980 had killed their aspirations. On the other hand one can conclude that Québeckers have accepted the notion of fence-sitting, and that not having decided to opt for separation in 1980 they will never decide to do so and are prepared to accept a continuing waste of time and money. Both interpretations are possible, and both are realistic enough. Each one of us makes a choice that appears to be instinctive but which is really the product of our conditioning and our past experiences.

The tactics adopted by the Parti Québecois in its lead-up to the referendum are transparent: to make people believe that the majority is in favour of sovereignty, from the Premier Jacques Parizeau who exudes an exuberant confidence, to Pierre Bourgault[1] who claims to have detected a great change in the mentality of Québeckers since 1980. Seeing and hearing this, the run-of-the-mill voter decides that he might as well "go with the flow" and be on the winning side. As tactics go this may not be a bad one since it may gather in some votes, except that it relies on our intellectual inadequacies, our tendency to trust what we see on the television, our lack of critical sense. Come on, make up your own minds!

If I no longer believe in the independence of Québec it doesn't mean that I have become a staunch federalist. The Rocky Mountains do not mean anything to me, and at the level of provincial politics, the cause of federalism is as badly defended by Daniel Johnson as independence is by Jacques Parizeau. Mr. Johnson is also guilty of fence-sitting. Thus when he tries to give an example he does not say "a Canadian living in Québec" but rather "a Québecois that is Canadian". Some may see this as a minor nuance, but I do not think so. A federalist must have the courage of his convictions even if it means risking the loss of a few votes. Certainly, one cannot accuse Québec politicians of rashness: even in their shortest speeches they try to please the greatest possible number of people. A federalist must see himself as a Canadian and declare himself in accordance with his convictions. If Mr. Johnson will not act accordingly, why should we believe any of his utterances? I am not referring here to his apparent lack of warmth and all the other elements that influence our perception of him: his words are his undoing.

[1] Pierre Bourgault an ardent nationalist and one of the "originals" of present-day Québecois separatism. An author and sometimes newspaper columnist, Bourgault was latterly employed as an advisor to Premier Jaques Parizeau until he delivered himself of threateningly negative remarks about the possible impact of anglophone and other minorities on the upcoming Québec referendum which resulted in his resignation.

I am not a federalist because the federalist position does not touch me at all. Québec remains a province not because it belongs to Canada but because its citizens refuse to take their own destiny in hand. The federalists are demanding a referendum in 1995. I do not think that it should take place because humiliation, if it does not kill, can still wound deeply.

I wonder who will really win the referendum? Not whether the "yes" side or the "no" side will win, but who of the population of Québec will genuinely benefit from this public consultation? This is an important question since our politicians claim that they are fighting the battle on our behalf. I don't think that anyone will win. If the "no" side wins we will find ourselves in the same situation as in 1980, with a majority government in the legislature but a loser nevertheless. The debate will continue and in fifteen or twenty years the question will re-surface and more millions (perhaps billions by then) will be wasted. This is not a case of investment, since political parties pay to be seen and heard, and there is no real return on this out-lay. A few votes, perhaps, are gained in exchange for large sums of money spent on commissions and consultations, on displays and posters, and nobody talks about it or seems to mind this flagrant waste.

If the "yes" side wins, the people will soon tire of the constant talk of negotiations and protests, of pilot-projects and sub-committees, of compromises and the exodus of the dissatisfied, to say nothing of the fact that the percentage of the vote will be seen as not having been high enough to warrant a move to sovereignty. There will be a lot of quib-bling over these percentages, especially since sovereignty will affect all the people, not only those who voted "yes". In a couple of weeks, at most in a month, no one will want to hear any more about sovereignty. But all of this is only for show since any searching discussion of the issues will again be avoided, just as it is being avoided now. Even if we ignore the general indifference that will follow the referendum, I am sure that a few years later nothing will have changed. The economic situation will not have changed for the better because Québec will have become sovereign, and since economics influence our morale, our worries and concerns will remain the same.

The only advantage that I see in the victory of the "yes" side is that we will stop talking about the sovereignty of Québec since we will be living it (and realizing that it is not heaven on earth). This is the logical and likely conclusion, although something tells me that the hatchet will never be truly buried. Knowing the Québecois I venture to predict that there will soon emerge a political party or a mass movement seeking re-unification with Canada. Who knows, maybe these people will win an election. Then, of course, they will hold a referendum on ending Québec sovereignty, and being good citizens of Québec we will vote: maybe…

THE MEDIA

I have been asking myself since the beginning of this adventure about the role of the media and the false information that they convey. I am not prepared to condemn the media wholesale for all the evils of society even if some are inclined to do so because I believe that it is time for the individual to assume some responsibility. The problem, as I see it, does not arise with the media but is due, rather, to a flagrant lack of critical sense. It doesn't really matter what the media present to us if we are able to stand back and assess the information that is being given to us. However, the tendency today is to accept what is being presented to us and, for lack of an alternate point of view, to take it at face value thus losing any sense of perspective.

That is why it is so important to have people develop their own critical sense not only in regard to what the media say but also in the way in which they see the world, since nothing is purely objective. Objectivity is an illusion since our choice of words influences the sense of what we are saying and eliminates any chance at being objective. In a wider perspective, the selection of what is published, shown or distributed as information transforms the reality both of readers and viewers. It is not that this information is somehow false, but simply that it is "selected". It is time, therefore, to stop blaming the media or others for our own inadequacies. They are the reflection of what we are, and it includes our lack of critical sense.

Those who, in their struggle against the general ambience of doubt and apathy, think that they can cleanse the media of their negative reporting of social problems inhabit a bubble of unreality. It is only when one has all the facts that one can teach oneself to decide wisely. Any attempt, therefore, to conceal the unpleasant elements of reality is more dangerous than showing only the dark side, and betrays a fascist predisposition to control the press, and with it, the electronic media as well.

Censoring violence in television, for example, while commendable in itself is also a futile endeavour. There have been many studies of the impact of violence on television viewers. Some of these studies have concluded that, indeed, violence in television programmes has made viewers more violent, while other studies advance the theory that, on the contrary, there is a cathartic release. In a curious coincidence it has been noted that during the hockey strike there were more incidents of domestic violence reported to the police. The problem seems to come not from television but from our inability to live in harmony in society. It has even been suggested by people shocked by television programmes that children killed a little girl while playing at Power Rangers. Those children were sick, and they were suffering from a lack of contact with reality; for them it wasn't a question of less violence on television, but a question of proper treatment for their malady.

In any case those seeking to curb violence on television are unbelievably ineffectual in their tactics. For example, when at the beginning of a film they announce that due to material of a violent or sexual nature the film is restricted to adults, they ensure that a young audience will be glued to their sets. We do not need a lengthy disquisition on the attraction of the forbidden to know that it appeals to people of all ages. Parental control does not enter into the discussion here since we know that children must learn to make informed choices on their own, and that they have to be left alone from time to time to do that. Constant parental supervision is not only utopian but is probably harmful to the child. It's folly to think that the little ones will see only that which is good for them if their parents do their job. One might even suggest that knowing what is going on out there may help them to develop a critical sense. If they inhabit a cocoon like little Care Bears with mummy protecting them from anger and violence and father supervising their games so that there is not the slightest chance of a disagreement, how will these children cope with the real world when they grow up? They simply won't be able to cope, and will turn out to be awkward and maladjusted.

Similarly and just as one does for television, there has been talk recently about parental supervision of toys. For a few years now, it has become customary to deplore the playing of war games, and parents who allow their children to have war toys have been considered as insensitive to this issue. But long before children's toys were a store-bought and manufactured commodity, children everywhere played cowboys and indians and cops and robbers. They made their guns out of suitably shaped branches and tied handkerchiefs around their faces, and played at shooting one another as violently as today. The only difference is that, then, we could not blame television for this. This was also before parents become obsessed with analysing in great detail what was good or not good for their kids, and before the parents forgot that what a child needs is care and love and a stable environment before reality, of which violence is a part, makes everything taboo.

The media are swamped by advertising of which they try to make art as if we are delighted to have shampoos or body cream pushed relentlessly at us; as if we do not pass the time during commercials surfing from channel to channel. It matters little how we react; advertising is all around us, and the experts console themselves by saying that if a commercial does not appeal to a person it is because it was not destined for that person. In other words, the advertisement was aimed at some other gullible consumer. Pause and think for a minute or two before an advertisement, and try to imagine the intellectual level of those to whom it is addressed. It is depressing, yet we continue to support these companies, to buy their products. Who is the sucker, then? We are taken for the fools that we are, and we ask for more, while we close our eyes and pretend all along that we cannot change anything.

EDUCATION

Before we begin any discussion on education it is necessary to define the term. What is the real goal of education? Is it to drill ourselves in a mindless learning of the procedures of societal life so that we can find a corner for ourselves, or is it the intention of education to make us as complete as possible as human beings and happy in our lives.

If we want our student population to be unthinking and cattle-like, either obedient or defying, and with no thought for anything other than to drink and have a good time, then we are on the right track. I don't want to be told that mindlessness is normal for the young generation, it is simply not true. If on the other hand we are committed to helping young people to realize their goals, then we have to restructure our way of thinking. This would mean putting the means of achieving their goals at their disposal. It does not mean that we have to push the young person to be best in their chosen area; it does mean, however, that we have to give the young as broadly based an education as possible buttressed by good and accurate information and enough of a challenge to motivate them towards real success. Course work should be set at a higher and more demanding level, and course materials should be better organized (there are instances at the CEGEP level when the same text is used and re-used in different courses, and while this may simplify matters for the students it also makes the experience uninteresting, useless and repetitious). The important point here is to raise the value of knowledge and learning. I also want to stress that this should be accomplished not by encouraging everyone to go in for university studies (university is not everybody's cup of tea, both in terms of capability and of interests), but by encouraging the young person to excel intellectually. Because knowledge and learning do not necessarily translate into promotion and more money on the job, does not make them irrelevant or superfluous. For those who have argued that the attainment of a certain level of general culture is useless for the average working person or factory employee, I would like to quote from Cyrano de Bergerac: "It is far more beautiful when it appears to be useless".

I also believe that we should open the doors to culture to everyone so that they can decide for themselves as to the use they want to make of the knowledge that will be placed at their finger tips. This process is necessarily undergone through education, and it is something that has failed in the system in Québec. Clearly the school does not have the mandate or the means to make everything available to the individual, but it should give him an idea of what is out there.

There is a tendency to blame the educational system in its entirety. But we must remember that our own people have devised this system, have made it work, and continue to make it work to this day. The system is not some kind of faceless and independent entity. It is what we have made it, and we should recognize our guilt and our responsibility in making it what it is.

Surely it is time to acknowledge the importance of education in society and to stop tinkering with its bits and pieces like a sorcerer's apprentice. We are not playing games with innocuous substances but with the lives of generations. After the teaching of the French language "by ear", we went on to hype the importance of "freedom"

above all else, then the idea that oral expression is para-
mount, then the notion that the teacher was there to be your
friend rather than to teach. In the name of the ideal of education for everyone (which was put in place too quickly
and without proper planning and reflection), we ended up
with a situation in which thousands of students were badly
taught. They came out with mediocre qualifications and we
proceeded to lower our standards to accomodate this level
of accomplishment. Since then things have gone steadily
downhill. I see only one solution: we have to change the
whole system radically and immediately.

I have had it pointed out to me that learning and education are not essential elements, and I have even heard it
suggested that they are not vitally linked with our continued existence as a people. However, in the words of a pro-
gramme enunciated by the Parti Québecois, "education,
research and the diffusion of culture (all closely linked) are
not only the prime condition of all development, but are the
guarantors of autonomy and even of the survival of soci-
eties". I use the words of others in this instance because it
is essential to understand the importance of education and
of culture, and I fear that if I use my own words again people will only see this as an opportunity to duck reality. I
want to serve notice on those who (perhaps for selfish reasons), deny the importance of learning for humanity, both
as individuals and as peoples. Just because I am the one
who is saying it does not make it false or inconsequential.

I have been reproached for advocating a return to the
old classical college system (it doesn't matter that I never
suggested it), which, annoyingly, put books on the banned
list. The point is that it doesn't take a great deal of intelligence to realize that a flawed system can be improved

without sweeping it away entirely. It is certainly a lot less risky than to demolish everything and to try to rebuild too quickly on the resulting ruins.

We should also stop making little marginal changes—I am thinking here of the minor shuffle in CEGEP programmes which was effected last year—and thinking that it will do. Generations were sacrificed because neither the schools nor the parents saw what was self-evident: that the children should be taught to better themselves and to excel beyond that which was offered in school. Quite the contrary, we have encouraged laziness. This must be acknowledged immediately and reforms begun at the elementary level first with a re-evaluation of teachers, and then onwards and upwards with other necessary reforms.

What holds for the elementary schools is also applicable to high schools and colleges. We must promote intellectual rigour. Freedom of thought is good but without guidance it ends up all over the place. The result of this lack of intellectual discipline is there for all to see. We have students who are disorganized in their thinking and who lack a practical sense. They hit the wall when they get to college or university where the ability to organize their time and efforts is all important, and where there is no one to tell them how to do it. Discipline is not a straight-jacket but a tool that allows the elaboration of more complex projects and thinking in a way which carries the effort beyond the simply passable. It also fights mental laziness and enables students to create and define (both by themselves and for themselves) attainable objectives which, in turn, are a source of great satisfaction. By lowering its standards and being undemanding, the school system has done away with challenge and motivation.

I am not convinced by the claim that I keep hearing that, as it is, a lot of students are experiencing difficulties even with existing lowered standards, and to raise these would cause them grief. Quite the contrary, I think that if success in school became more difficult students would be forced to improve themselves to perform at a higher level, and they would do it. Maybe they would not be up there at the head of the class, but I do not think that they would be that far behind either. Many of the ones that we look upon as dunces and under-achievers are students who have not been challenged to make the effort to work harder. Sixty per cent is good enough for them, and if the standard is lowered to fifty they adapt quite readily to that too and float at about the same level as before. Many of the criteria that go into the determining of grades are purely psychological. Those who would deny this like to insist that some children are born stupid, but I do not believe it. One can, of course, convince those children of this, but I prefer to think that children are born with, more or less, the same abilities, and I cannot see how their grades would change simply because the standards had been raised. It is likelier that intellectual discipline would improve their ability to do well-organized school work of quality. It goes without saying that this reform goes hand in hand with an emphasis on the value of knowledge itself since a raising of standards by itself will not change anything, the problem being more profoundly ingrained than we imagine. For once we have to change things at their core and not rely on superficial tinkering with surface values only.

I am also calling for a re-examination of the system that drives our CEGEP's. These do not fulfill the functions intended for them or, for that matter, functions that could be structured otherwise. For example we might think of a sixth year of high school as well as of a pre-university year. This would encourage student exchanges between our system and other systems, especially since there is no equivalent of our CEGEP elsewhere.

Most CEGEP programmes are so ill-defined and so badly structured that the contents of a course may not only vary from college to college but also, quite eccentrically, from instructor to instructor. Within a large course framework the instructor teaches, pretty much, what pleases him or her. It has been possible to take a course in philosophy under four different rubrics and find oneself studying essentially the same material; or, on the other hand, take a course described as the "history of philosophy" and end up studying classical philosophy up to the Middle Ages and no farther; or to end up with courses of pure theory, all being predicated on the whims and interests of the instructor. The result is an educational pattern without rhyme or reason and one in which the material is quickly forgotten, probably right after the examination. To compound this problem the instructor has a great deal of latitude in grading. Some never give more than eighty per cent, others reward lavishly with near-perfect grades. The system is thrown in disarray and there is no basis for comparison when students apply for admission to university. Simply put, this is unjust and inadequate.

The CEGEP was a stopgap measure designed to hold for a while young students who did not have a clear idea about their future (rendered all that much more painful now that they have grave doubts about having any future at all). These students hesitate between technical training, a university education or just dropping out completely. Since we have not trained them to make intelligent choices we cannot rush them to a decision. Our solution is to offer them a period of transition in which to earn a general diploma. In reality (and in many cases) this becomes two years of drinking beer and carousing at parties rather than two years of serious study. Oftentimes courses require little effort, and it is permissible to flunk a few anyway. They become confirmed in the mental laziness that we have taught them and which, incidentally, is also our affliction; they never mature and they go away without having understood the purpose of education in the first place. In presenting this example I have deliberately skirted those who may have to work up to twenty hours a week in order to make ends meet. These form a minority. The larger number work, if at all, to buy a car, to have money for outings or treats. Some work so as to save for university. Many, however, are "lost" in the process either for lack of a challenge or because "real" life manages to sidetrack them. They have not forgotten what it is that they set out to do, it is only that they have chosen to postpone it... year after year. The CEGEP becomes their second home (although most of the time they have to go outside to smoke, which pleases me). They have become, in effect, what we have taught them; and they refuse to grow up.

The young generation, unable to write properly, is massively disinterested in schooling. Unfortunately, our schools instead of pushing the young students to meet higher standards have resigned themselves to meeting the sinking levels of their charges.

It has been said often enough that the slogan "Education for All" was a mistake that led us into terrible error and excess in which oral expression was privileged at the expense of everything else. Education begins before the formal process of schooling and continues beyond it. It requires the cooperation of the child and the help of the parents. Later, the student carries on for himself, and I do not mean doing his homework, but wanting to know and understand things beyond the school's curriculum which is so undemanding that to be satisfied with it is to run the risk of becoming dull-witted. By raising the level of education received at home we face the prospect of improving our schools which will have to reach higher if the calibre of student improves steadily. I hate to think that this will be possible only in an ideal world since we seem to be bogged down in the mentality of the happily ignorant. Small wonder that children in school mock and taunt those of their peers who like to read or who are straight A students. This is not simple-minded jealousy, the kids are mirroring the attitudes that they see at home. That is why reform of the school system must begin at home, although I doubt that it will happen since not everyone recognizes that education and learning are great advantages in our world.

It is also fashionable to blame our teachers and instructors for this state of affairs. But what can we expect of them? We send them a clear message as to what we think of them and their role by paying them ridiculous salaries. If we count the number of hours that they spend on the education of our children it comes out to be less important than our entertainment or sports or humour since we compensate people in those fields much more generously than we reward those to whom we have entrusted forty hours a week in the lives of our children. This is a regrettable choice that society has made, and while I am not asking for an increase in teacher's salaries in these difficult times, I do think that a more equitable system of compensation must be arrived at if we are to recognize the social importance of the teaching profession. It may very well be too late to do anything about this.

In the meantime while we wait for parents and children to change and for the educational system to be transformed, the poor student is dying of boredom in the classroom. This is not the fault of the teacher, but is a problem with varied and mixed levels of attainment and potential among the students, some of whom are forced to sit and wait while the class catches up. So, they dream of "jumping" a grade or of going to an alternative school, something that is not always possible for them. This is the process of levelling from the bottom which is an everyday affair in our schools. We apply the brakes with the more gifted (and they are not all geniuses, just kids who have a passion to know) holding them back until they are sick and bored with school. Becoming discouraged, they succumb to mental laziness and discover that when one is gifted one can coast without much effort and beat others without trying. One forgets one's ambitions and one loses one's motivation. I wonder what happens to these students in later life, and while I do not know if they are able to recover their drive I am sure that their potential is warped by their experience at school. Yet there is a fairly simple solution: create accelerated classes. Or, on the other hand, challenge the more able with a heavier work load and make more demands on their capabilities. Some teachers do this already with some success, but what is called for here is a uniform policy to serve the needs of the gifted student. Such a policy would apply chiefly at the elementary level, but it would also be useful at the beginning of high school. Following such an introduction, students should be able to take charge of their own studies. There are other problems, of course. For example it happens frequently that teachers are not happy to have their students tell them that the material being studied is not challenging enough. In these situations students are not sure as to how to react. They strive to be independent and self-directing but are too often frustrated by a lack of challenge or the envy of fellow-students that traps them in inaction. Adults who fail to understand the nature of the problem refer to it as a crisis of adolescence, but, nevertheless, it is something that is very difficult to overcome.

The school, therefore, frustrates and blocks those who would advance and damages those who are not up to the level of more gifted class-mates. At least this is how it feels for those of us who have had to live through it. We seem to have the freedom of choice but it takes a while before we learn to take advantage of it. School becomes a negative experience although it is what we make it, and it will continue to be, at best, a mediocre thing until enough people revolt against the status quo. In all of this we must not lose sight of the fact that it is every individual's responsibility to see to his or her education and, even more importantly, their culture. We may complain that schools fail to instill in us a love of reading, but there is nothing to prevent us from developing the habit of reading independent of what we do in school. If we decide not to develop good reading habits it is because we do not feel encouraged to do so since it is well-known that it is much harder to become a habitual reader of books when one is older than if one has been encouraged and nurtured in that habit from a young age by one's parents and others who are in positions of influence. This is why a child growing up in a household with books and seeing parents who read will not have to be urged to read but will likely fall into the habit quite naturally.

If I insist a lot on the importance of starting to read at a young age it is because reading enhances one's sense of language, imagination and independence of thought, all of which will help greatly in the development of a critical sensibility vis à vis the world which surrounds us. Like many other things that shape us, reading is an individual undertaking which stems from ourselves and our families. This is why it is so important to realize that we cannot blame our system of education as if it were a personal thing with a will of its own.

We do have a system created by us which encourages mental laziness especially where language is concerned. We cannot expect that the school system will turn everyone into an accomplished writer, but, unfortunately, the system produces people without any writing skills. I believe that writing ability is more likely to come from the solitary act of reading than from all the cramming that school may do, although, in the final analysis it matters little where the rudiments are learned so long as they are acquired at an early age. It is then up to the school to make sure that suitable standards of learning and skill are reached so that its certificate is a true measure of achievement. This is a point that has to be addressed. A telling example comes to mind.

Last September Le Devoir reported that the french test given to the current crop of graduating students at CEGEP's had produced better results than in past years. There was a lot of satisfied discussion about this test but I, for one, would like to tell the truth about it, and it is not the "truth" we hear from officials in education. The so-called test was a joke. It was ill-conceived, poorly evaluated and its results are ridiculous and without any merit whatsoever.

Students were asked to write a five hundred word essay stating their well-argued opinion on the following perennial topic: "What do you think of nuclear energy, or of the salaries of hockey players, or of current soap operas, or whatever?" Well, not having trained them to think critically we now want them to write an essay of reasoned opinion without caring too much how or why they have arrived at this opinion. To help them along we have allowed them to bring along two writing tools: either a dictionary and/or a grammar or a table of conjugation. It matters little, apparently, that in their everyday lives they rarely use a dictionary or any other writing tool, which is to say that the test does not demonstrate their writing skill but their ability to rummage about in a reference work... And even so, many managed to fail the test!

Furthermore, I want to comment on the test as an instrument for evaluating the ability of students to write in French. What it does is to force students into following inflexible rules of writing that have been drilled into them by their teachers. It is formula writing which favours short sentences, stereotyped structuring and clichés of phrasing so that there is no sense of individual style. I know what I am talking about. I wrote the test using the simplest constructions in order to avoid breaking the rules and failing. I got ninety-nine per cent and I am ashamed of it! Ashamed of having played the Ministry's game and of having satisfied its automaton-like examiners who, if they encounter a sentence longer than two lines, consider it to be an error. I don't think that future winners of literary awards are going to do well in this test.

One third of those taking the test fail it, and when these

statistics are released the public concludes that the test is too hard and that it would be better to lower the grading standard. I think not. What we have to do is to change the test fundamentally and to train those marking it not to become obsessed with minor points of style. If, after this, a third of the students continues to fail, too bad for them! Surely, if they want to go on to university or, at least, to earn a college diploma they have to learn how to write properly, and this without Mummy on the spot to help out and their teachers following their every move. At the age of eighteen or nineteen it is not too much to expect the student to abandon the passivity and indifference in which he or she has been schooled, and to take charge of the situation, something that is closer to real life. It is sad enough that students get into the CEGEP without really knowing how to put one word after another. To favour and to try and help at any price those who are destined to fail in any case does no one any favours. They will get into university and months will be lost before they discover their inadequacies and gaps in their learning. Our society would be much better off with a system that is genuinely demanding and without any of the well-meaning illusions current today. I am all in favour of helping the disadvantaged and the weak, but I am convinced that it is wrong to encourage them to think that they are somehow up to the mark. We have done too much of this already.

As I have said earlier, it is not in school that we learn our language but through reading to which we become accustomed through our parents and our social milieu. Attempts in school to overcome a lack of preparation on the part of students by drilling them in rules of grammar does not really help because rules are not as important as an understanding of how a language functions. Rules learnt by heart for purposes of examination and forgotten the next day are of no use to the student. A true understanding of a language is the result of use and practice over time.

Low standards are self-defeating and do untold damage to the student. Recently the newspapers were crowing about the fact that high school students who were in the habit of spending six to ten hours a week reading were also succeeding much better in their studies. Naturally, and I know this from personal experience, reading does no harm, but I am somewhat doubtful of the way in which these facts have been presented and interpreted. They compared the performance of two groups of students (those who read a lot and those who were moderate readers) in a French test administered by the Ministry of Education to recent high school graduates. The findings were that those who read a lot were generally more successful than their fellow-students: they scored sixty-nine per cent compared with sixty-one per cent for the others. And we are proud of these results! As far as I am concerned sixty-nine per cent is nothing about which we should be self-congratulatory. After five years of studying and reading French almost on a daily basis, scoring sixty-nine per cent in a writing test is not an acceptable result. As a matter of fact it is something of which we should be ashamed. But, according to the survey, quite a few people were pleased and relieved by these results!

Yet our system of education enables students with only a slight effort to score higher than a measly sixty-nine per cent. In being satisfied with this level of performance we send out a clear message to all who will listen: mediocrity is good enough for us.

Scores of sixty-nine per cent in French, even for those who read a lot, are a symptom of something more widespread and more serious. I cannot help but conclude that television is having a long-term effect on us. The problem is grave enough to give us pause. It is very likely that those tested who were supposed to spend six to ten hours a week reading also spent two or three times that amount of time watching television, although I hesitate to place all the blame on television which has its good points as well. We have to admit, though, that television is a seductive medium which it is very difficult to resist despite the claptrap that is often presented on it. On the one hand the public gets to view, consciously or otherwise, what it wants or what it prefers, except that many of the programmes are quite silly and are watched purely out of habit. That is another side of our intellectual laziness as a result of which we fall, too readily and without reflection, into a mindless and passive habit of self-entertainment.

Here is something that was overheard recently: "Pis là tu downloader ta file pis tu fais edit". Three English words in a short sentence! Would it not be better if we spoke English rather than to bastardize French in this fashion? And please don't get me wrong, I am not suggesting that we abandon the French language which I love dearly with all its faults. Why not speak two languages instead of pretending to speak one language while borrowing sixty per cent of our vocabulary from the other… There is a time and a place for everything. One can elect to speak the language which is most appropriate for the particular use to which it is being put. This is not abandoning a language but using it in a way in which its strengths are best utilized for the purposes at hand. Computer-related communication is the most obvious example since English is best adapted to its uses and has become a universal language regardless of the user's native tongue. It also seems to me that using English for computer terminology is preferable to using French which is gradually being destroyed little by little when we import foreign terms into it and forget that phrases such as "downloader une file" in which two words out of three are English is not French.

I am not extolling the use of English because it is the language of the invader or because anglophones are supposedly superior to us. No, we should not adopt a language because of some kind of cowardice or because of a sense of inferiority. We should learn to use it because, like it or not, it is something of us. There is only one caveat, we must choose rationally and we must settle, once and for all, our feeling of being inferior vis à vis the English.

Purists of the French language may reproach me for saying that we should sometimes abandon French in favour of a language better suited to reality. But French has already lost much ground and it is not at all certain that the process can be reversed. The most powerful proof of this development lies in our daily life where in almost all areas well-spoken French is viewed askance. What we have to do is to make sure that we employ correct usage; that we avoid colloquial contractions; that we steer clear of Québecois joual, all of which, of course, if you were to suggest it would have people looking at you as if you were some strange animal. It is a rare exception today when someone can recite French poetry and employ correct pronunciation in doing so. Saying "Comment vas-tu?" instead of "Ça va?"; respecting the syntax of the French language (as a matter of fact knowing that such a thing exists!) is imme-

diately seen as being pretentious or, as they say colloquial-
ly in French, "farting higher than the hole".

When we fail to use our own language properly, when
we barter it thoughtlessly as much as possible for another,
when we are prejudiced against those of us who dare to
speak French correctly, we are guilty of a lack of respect
towards something that is vitally part of us and happens to
define us. We are, then, ultimately guilty of a lack of self-
respect. But we go merrily on, shrugging things off since
they seem to us to be only trifles. "relax, man, there's no
problem…" Yeah, right!

Before we take it for granted that we have mastery of
our own language in a way such as to allow us to open ourselves to the world by encouraging the study of other languages we have to give primacy to French above all other
languages so as to ensure that it does not disappear. Since
the promotion of the French language is undertaken within
narrow and precise cultural contexts, this activity has little
impact on the general public, which means, in effect, that
the problem is not addressed globally, and that we continue to tread water. We delude ourselves by pushing back the
day of reckoning, always lowering our standards in the
hope that we can declare our language alive and well, while
its use continues to decline and its quality deteriorates. In
doing this we simply put off the problem to a later date
hoping against hope that it will never arrive as we take
pleasure from our mediocre knowledge of French (and,
occasionally of English), content in our mediocrity which
cuts us off from hundreds of other pressing realities.

Contrary to what many believe, the independence of
Québec will not solve the problems of the French language.
If the people of Québec are not particularly interested in

the French language now, what is there to say that they will be more interested when they inhabit their own country. It is being said that as a country Québec will have to communicate with other countries and that, in order to be understood it will have to use French correctly. It should be noted, though, that English is the language of international usage while relations between countries, whether in trade or diplomacy, are limited to a tiny minority.

To my mind, the real problem is not that an anglophone presence completely surrounds the French fact. The problem lies with francophones who do not care about their native language, who have given up on it or who speak it badly, or who do not have the intellectual will to cultivate and maintain it even when they are called upon to learn or to use other languages.If one knows a language but is prepared to let it go little by little, one regresses. If we allow this to happen in the case of language, then it is probably true, as well, in a larger cultural sense.

What it becomes, then, is an acceptance that the human being has gone as far as s/he can, and that the time has come to regress back to the cave, forgetting, bit by bit, the real accomplishments of mankind.

The survival of the French language, if it will survive at all, is something that depends on a deeply-felt personal conviction of each individual. A lot of time and effort is lost by trying to put the blame on others, and, not infrequently, by choosing the easiest target: the English. We accuse them of being racist, of exploiting us, of despising us. These are powerful labels and very handy in blaming others. But the anglophones have behaved in exactly the same way as we would have done if we had been in their place. If they have succeeded economically and have been rich longer than we it is because while they were enriching themselves we were at mass or struggling to clear some Godforsaken corner of this land. What's the point of being paranoid about all this today? Languages are not in conflict, it is human beings who confront one another. We have lost enough time, perhaps we should look at ourselves first before we insult them. We will see then that we are experiencing difficulty in operating in our own language, and if we do not bestir ourselves we will have acquiesced in the disappearance of French which once had a place in America. This is not a great tragedy, except that it is a decision that should be made consciously and deliberately rather than by letting things slide.

On the Thoughtlessness of Human Beings in General

The search for a religion at all costs which is widespread in the history of humanity strikes me as symptomatic of an unease that may be inherent in our kind (even if I hope that it is not so). The reason for this quest is not clear to me. In the beginning mankind did not understand its world and it had to invent gods to explain that which it could not explain by itself. Today, other than the question of the meaning of life, the single issue that remains a mystery is what follows death, is it nothingness or is it something else? So, the fact that people turn to religion is entirely understandable, although a philosophy of life based on some straightforward ideas and without the burden of dogma and illusions would serve just as well. Then why, I ask myself, are we witnessing this multiplying growth of new religions and sects? There is a recognition in Québec that since the rejection of the Catholic Church we have been living in a spiritual void. But spirituality does not have to be limited to religion. Why should we seek to replace one crutch with another? The answer is neither clear nor simple, but it does demonstrate certain facts.

Namely:
1. Human beings have no self-confidence;
2. We prefer to believe anything (or almost anything) so long as we do not have to admit our ignorance and our inability to change things;
3. We do not learn from our mistakes.

There is every indication that human beings are weak in their intelligence and that we do not know how to use what little intelligence we do have. I am not convinced by the argument that we have made progress since if that were to be the case why is it that we have not advanced much in our understanding of intangible things? What does mankind really do other than to make tools and instruments and perfect them? We have been doing this for thousands of years, and as a result of that we have heated caves and we wash more often! That seems to be the only difference.

Forgive me if I am unkind and say that man today is a lazier creature. Once upon a time, and because he had no other option, man hunted in order to sustain himself. Today there is no need to hunt, and man prefers to wallow mindlessly rather than use his free time to improve himself. This is not said because I despise humanity; I too like to laze about, except that there is a difference between laziness and stupidity, and I believe that it is stupid of us not to accept the responsibility for our actions and try to put the blame on someone else. We do it all the time. We have exchanged our Catholic perspective which taught us that things were as God wanted them to be for another outlook which has not made anything clearer. Now it's the government that is stupid (although it was elected partly by those who complain…), and taxes are too high (although we were happy with the lifestyle that we enjoyed not so long ago and which has brought us to the present-day condition…), and, of course, it is never the individual voter who is to blame. What appears to be a problem of definition and semantics affects how we see the world.

...SPEAKING OF PEOPLE HERE, ESPECIALLY.
Blaming everybody and all institutions has become a
national sport and, in many cases, it influences falsely our
judgement both as individuals and as a society. Again, this
year, we have been treated to the story of cigarette smuggling. The real problem arises when a society chooses to
become preoccupied with the effects and not the causes of
its malaise. We had a simple issue. Cigarettes were heavily
taxed and people took to smuggling them and selling them
illegally at a profit. The result was that those authorised
and licensed to sell tobacco products lost a lot of money.
This became a huge issue and resulted in demonstrations
and illegal public sales and the involvement of the RCMP.
The illegal activity of smuggling was soon forgotten in this
hubbub, and taxes were lowered in order to help the sales
of legitimate businesspeople. Is that a solution for anything? Not likely. The problem has been shuffled off to a
later date. Smokers continue to pollute the air, and smuggling continues to thrive. At least we don't hear about it
any more, we seem to be saying...

Perhaps it is because we are human beings first and
Québeckers second that we tend to forget quickly... I don't
want to get into a set of elaborate historical examples, especially since others have been much better at it than I, but I
do want to take this opportunity to recall a couple of recent
instances that are relevant to what I am saying.

About two years ago it was decided, with the help of large
government subsidies, to open the Museum of Humour. Not
very far away, the Théâtre du Nouveau Monde was in danger

---

[1] Théâtre du Nouveau-Monde has received more than one million dollars—$532,000 in 1994-1995 and $532,000 in 1995-1996— from The
Canada Council in support of its operations. It has also, reportedly,
received additional assistance from the provincial government subse-
quent to this statement by Ms. Jutras.

—and continues to be in danger—of collapsing on the heads of its audience, while other theatres are having to give away free tickets in order to fill their auditoria. We couldn't have cared less about their problems but chose instead to pour piles of money into the new museum on the pretext that it would be profitable. But problems developed almost immediately. Ticket prices were set too high, and while the consumer public may have wanted to be amused, it was not prepared to buy its laughs at such a high price. A few months later the museum had to close its doors—temporarily, only to reopen with a great deal of pomp and ceremony. Artists took up the museum's cause, special activities were organized to support it, the price of tickets was lowered to a reasonable level. Except for one thing, though. A lot of the government's (that is our) money was pumped into this monument to humour of which many people did not approve, and we won't get any of that money back.

Also, a couple of years ago, the minister responsible, Lucienne Robillard[1] proposed a plan to reform our system of CEGEP's which, by the way, badly need to be reformed even if this idea of Madam Robillard was debatable. Students were up in arms as soon as the project of reform was proposed. There was talk of a general strike and calls for protests and demonstrations. Students' associations called meetings which were packed with militant participants. However, in many CEGEP's all that happened was a tame study day. Where were the students' associations when the reforms were accepted and became the reality rather than a topic for militant debate? We saw professors, but the students did not speak up at all publicly, and simply

---

[1] Prior to winning a seat in a by-election and being appointed Minister of Labour in Prime Minister Chrétien's government, Lucienne Robillard had served in the defeated provincial administration of Daniel Johnson.

ceased their protests. Now the issue that exercises student imaginations is the question of the reform of social programmes[1] some of which will have an impact upon student lives. Greatly upset by this prospect, students travelled in large numbers to Ottawa. With what result? They looked and behaved like savages throwing Kraft Dinner at Human Resources Minister Lloyd Axworthy. Mind you, I have absolutely nothing against a protest, but I disapprove of the methods employed. I wonder if the situation will develop similarly to what transpired when Minister Robillard implemented her reforms. Minister Axworthy's reforms are only in the planning stage; are we going to behave as we did earlier when the time comes to fight the implementation of these plans? Our capacity for indignation fades rapidly... Human beings are weak and seem to have invented forgetfulness as a tactic in order to be able to hold their heads high in their absurd pride.

By denying the truth and avoiding clear thinking we have made it possible for hypocrisy to become central to our system. While no one is prepared to admit it, it is nevertheless true that we do not really care about what happens in Bosnia, in Rwanda or in India. Of course thousands of people die there of hunger, injury, sickness and neglect and, of course, it is horrible and we should have the honesty to admit that we do not really care. The public stares vacantly at its televisions used as it is to images of children too weak to fight off the flies that plague them and of men and women mutilated and crying out in pain. These televiewers do not ask themselves what they can do to help

---

[1] This is a reference to the announcement by the Federal Government made shortly after the election of Prime Minister Chrétien and his Liberal administration that the Ministry of Human Resources Development would be undertaking a review of social programmes with a view to making recommendations to the Federal Cabinet for certain reforms necessitated by fiscal stringencies in the Federal budget.

(should they send money when they do not have any, and who knows what percentage gets through to the needy...). So they wait for the regional news; news about the economy and the security of their jobs; or a sports bulletin so that they can plan their evening of television. This apathy is total and real and it has become the norm in our behaviour. And to those who exclaim that I am mad or extreme in these judgements I say: "Do you think that all these horrors would go on for long if people really cared?' The invasion of Kuwait was quickly stopped by the Americans not only because of the importance of Kuwaiti oil, but also because of the impact of this oil on the daily lives of Americans. Bosnia on the other hand has very little effect on our lives. We shed a tear from time to time when you want to feel responsible and good. Then shopping takes over and you forget all about it. The physical closeness of events to our lives determines the degree of interest that we have in these events, but a direct link is much more telling and demanding of our attention. Yet we continue to close our eyes, to live in a kind of 'pretend' ignorance, stupid but contented. I can't accept it.

If you think that I am wrong to believe that we are addicted to props and crutches that keep us away from the hard facts of reality, then think of astrology. Think of characters like Jojo and all the success that is possible with schemes that swindle without any recourse to fact or science. People are only too happy to pay five dollars a minute to be able to speak to so-called psychics who tell them what numbers to play in the lottery. Nobody thinks to ask these psychics why they do not play these numbers for their own benefit. Surely it's not professional ethics that stands in their way! And all of this is legal, too. Let's bear in mind that astrology is not a science, and that no bit of astrological hocus pocus has ever stood up to scientific scrutiny. Worse still, astrology has not changed in two thousand years in spite of the fact that all other sciences have undergone change and development. In all this time astrology has insisted that it has the **TRUTH,** and it has not moved to adapt to changing times. The constellations of the zodiac have shifted, but astrologers have not taken this into account so that if they say that you are a Libra you are, in reality, a Virgo. Oops!

Even so, thousands of people continue to believe in this superstition and spend money on it and are swindled daily. You may think that reading your horoscope in the paper doesn't do any harm, but it does perpetuate the silliness and the mindlessness of which we are all victims. The real problem is not that astrology is out there and that we lend ourselves willingly to it. The matter for concern is that the too ready acceptance by the public of this kind of quackery suggests a deeper problem in our society which I have been trying to identify and attack, and which many others are trying to deny.

Another example of our intellectual poverty and our inclination to occupy ourselves with anything but the sad facts of our situation was the obsessive attention paid to the marriage of Céline Dion[1]. Whatever one may think of her talent, nothing justifies the attention that was paid by the public and the media to this event. It was almost as if on that day on December the 17TH, 1994, the world had ceased to

[1] Céline Dion, a popular female vocalist, was married with great fanfare and showmanship in Nôtre Dame Church in Montréal to her longtime manager. The wedding was preserved for posterity on film and in a lavishly produced instant book of photographs which reportedly sold half a million copies mostly to Québeckers. The mania and hype surrounding this event had people camping outside the church in the early hours of the morning in order to catch a glimpse of their "Star".

turn. All the television stations fought for scraps[2] of information, while bus loads of admiring fans had travelled from the far corners of the Province to gawk at the singer leaving the church clad in a fur stole that had cost the lives of fifteen mink.

Of course she is a star, and has many admirers and married her manager, but nothing can explain the excesses to which people were moved. Three weeks after the wedding the magazines were still talking about the "marriage of the princess" and "the price of fame" undaunted by the basest clichés of journalism. The first printing of the marriage 'album' was sold out in a matter of a few hours as if it was of vital importance. The hungry will throw themselves on the smallest scrap of food no matter if its rotten; we have thrown ourselves at this 'album' just as we throw ourselves collectively at gossip papers that supposedly purvey information in the form of stories about our "stars". It doesn't matter that such behaviour—for that matter even more excessive manifestations of it—may flourish elsewhere. If the Americans jump off bridges it doesn't mean that we have to imitate them; and if they do the intellectual equivalent it doesn't mean that we have to follow suit or to lead. The lives of "stars" enable the public to live vicariously dream lives that are better than their own. They prefer illusion! Dreaming may not be so bad in itself because it gives us hope, but opting for illusion is harmful because it drugs us into a state of oblivion. And where does that lead us? It leads us to where we are today: a terrible absence of clear-mindedness, a refusal to see things as they are, and bad faith in the face of reality.

[2] The reason for what proved to be an unseemly scramble for bits of information was that exclusive "rights" to film and telecast the wedding had been pre-sold to one television network effectively freezing out the rest of the media in the midst of what was a publicity frenzy.

Part Three

It has been made abundantly clear to me that for some it didn't matter at all whether I stayed or left. That's fine. This was not the most important concern that I had when I advanced my ideas. Where I decide to live eventually is nobody's business since it will have no bearing on your lives. It would have been easy just to get out of Québec and forget about all the things that I have been trying to say. People do it all the time. It only serves to prove what I have been at pains to denounce: our tendency to take the easy way out intellectually. Our mental laziness, the existence of which we deny, only proves my point.

I dream of a place where knowledge and learning are valued; where people speak four or five languages simply for the intellectual wealth that this provides. A place where summer entertainment does not sell out at the expense of classical theatre and traditional presentations that are in danger of folding or falling in on their sparse audiences. A place where potential is nurtured and not discouraged, where education is not an instrument of levelling to a lower common denominator, where people read and write because it is a good and normal thing to do. But that is not sufficient. I would also want a people that assumes its share of responsibilities and does not hide behind a screen in order to avoid discussing those responsibilities which they cannot avoid, a people that will stop blaming one another but will move forward to better things.

I have the impression that human beings from childhood until death change only in appearance. They grow physically in size; they gain weight, but they remain always irresponsible, apprehensive and full of prejudice. Above all, they are imbued with pride which prevents them from seeing their own weaknesses and failings. They see the inadequacies of their neighbours and of their spouse readily enough, and of other countries, but their own, never! Adults and children alike have read *The Little Prince*[1] and remember him saying "I am responsible for my rose", but they have never grasped its meaning beyond the primary level.

I have heard a specialist in Russian culture say that Russians are always dismayed by the portrait of them created by Chekhov in his plays. They are prompted to think that if they are as shown then they should make an effort to change. Québeckers, on the other hand when they see *Les Belles Soeurs* laugh at these portrayals of boorish characters and console themselves with the thought that it is only a play. After all, are we not more intelligent, kindlier and more at ease with ourselves than those people portrayed on the stage? To really get the meaning of the author's intention, they would have to think, and that is asking too much. Instead of reflecting on the meaning of the play, they are amused. They laugh at these lonely and miserable women, these poor people deprived and disadvantaged in every way without pausing to consider in what other way they could be relating to the play.

I have also been told that the place of which I dream is a myth, and that I am naive and a romantic. Of course I know that nothing is ever perfect, but I also believe that there are places on this earth where I would be more at ease. It does not mean that this other place will be perfect or extraordinary in some way, just that it will suit me. And if after having lived in various places and having searched without finding what I am looking for I decide that I need

[1] A modern-day fable, read by young and old alike, by Antoine de Saint Exupery (1900-1944), a French aviator and adventurer, and originally published in French as Le Petit Prince in 1943 a year before Exupery was lost in aerial combat.

a desert island, I will find one. I do not believe that happiness is found only in us since that is a half-truth. We are never totally susceptible to the things that surround us nor totally independent of them. Thus Québec which has made me has also made me dissatisfied with what it has to offer.

While it is true that the life of the intellect is a solitary one, it can, nevertheless, be shared when circumstances allow it. If the drive to forge ahead is an internal one, still it benefits from the help it receives from outside sources. For, you see, like you, I am still only a child.